MW01113518

"After utilizing toolkits from The Art of Service, I was able to identify threats within my organization to which I was completely unaware. Using my team's knowledge as a competitive advantage, we now have superior systems that save time and energy."

"As a new Chief Technology Officer, I was feeling unprepared and inadequate to be successful in my role. I ordered an IT toolkit Sunday night and was prepared Monday morning to shed light on areas of improvement within my organization. I no longer felt overwhelmed and intimidated, I was excited to share what I had learned."

"I used the questionnaires to interview members of my team. I never knew how many insights we could produce collectively with our internal knowledge."

"I usually work until at least 8pm on weeknights. The Art of Service questionnaire saved me so much time and worry that Thursday night I attended my son's soccer game without sacrificing my professional obligations."

"After purchasing The Art of Service toolkit, I was able to identify areas where my company was not in compliance that could have put my job at risk. I looked like a hero when I proactively educated my team on the risks and presented a solid solution."

"I spent months shopping for an external consultant before realizing that The Art of Service would allow my team to consult themselves! Not only did we save time not catching a consultant up to speed, we were able to keep our company information and industry secrets confidential."

"Everyday there are new regulations and processes in my industry. The Art of Service toolkit has kept me ahead by using AI technology to constantly update the toolkits and address emerging needs."

"I customized The Art of Service toolkit to focus specifically on the concerns of my role and industry. I didn't have to waste time with a generic self-help book that wasn't tailored to my exact situation."

"Many of our competitors have asked us about our secret sauce. When I tell them it's the knowledge we have in-house, they never believe me. Little do they know The Art of Service toolkits are working behind the scenes."

"One of my friends hired a consultant who used the knowledge gained working with his company to advise their competitor. Talk about a competitive disadvantage! The Art of Service allowed us to keep our knowledge from walking out the door along with a huge portion of our budget in consulting fees."

"Honestly, I didn't know what I didn't know. Before purchasing The Art of Service, I didn't realize how many areas of my business needed to be refreshed and improved. I am so relieved The Art of Service was there to highlight our blind spots."

"Before The Art of Service, I waited eagerly for consulting company reports to come out each month. These reports kept us up to speed but provided little value because they put our competitors on the same playing field. With The Art of Service, we have uncovered unique insights to drive our business forward."

"Instead of investing extensive resources into an external consultant, we can spend more of our budget towards pursuing our company goals and objectives…while also spending a little more on corporate holiday parties."

"The risk of our competitors getting ahead has been mitigated because The Art of Service has provided us with a 360-degree view of threats within our organization before they even arise."

OT operational technology
Complete Self-Assessment Guide

Notice of rights

You are licensed to use the Self-Assessment contents in your presentations and materials for internal use and customers without asking us - we are here to help.

All rights reserved for the book itself: this book may not be reproduced or transmitted in any form by any means, electronic, mechanical, photocopying, recording, or otherwise, without the prior written permission of the publisher.

The information in this book is distributed on an "As Is" basis without warranty. While every precaution has been taken in the preparation of the book, neither the author nor the publisher shall have any liability to any person or entity with respect to any loss or damage caused or alleged to be caused directly or indirectly by the instructions contained in this book or by the products described in it.

Trademarks

Many of the designations used by manufacturers and sellers to distinguish their products are claimed as trademarks. Where those designations appear in this book, and the publisher was aware of a trademark claim, the designations appear as requested by the owner of the trademark. All other product names and services identified throughout this book are used in editorial fashion only and for the benefit of such companies with no intention of infringement of the trademark. No such use, or the use of any trade name, is intended to convey endorsement or other affiliation with this book.

Copyright © by The Art of Service
https://theartofservice.com
support@theartofservice.com

Table of Contents

About The Art of Service   10

Included Resources - how to access   10
Purpose of this Self-Assessment   12
How to use the Self-Assessment   13
OT operational technology
Scorecard Example   15
OT operational technology
Scorecard   16

BEGINNING OF THE
SELF-ASSESSMENT: 17
CRITERION #1: RECOGNIZE   18

CRITERION #2: DEFINE: 30

CRITERION #3: MEASURE: 47

CRITERION #4: ANALYZE: 62

CRITERION #5: IMPROVE: 78

CRITERION #6: CONTROL: 95

CRITERION #7: SUSTAIN: 108
OT operational technology and Managing Projects, Criteria
for Project Managers: 133
1.0 Initiating Process Group: OT operational technology   134

1.1 Project Charter: OT operational technology   136

1.2 Stakeholder Register: OT operational technology   138

1.3 Stakeholder Analysis Matrix: OT operational technology
                                                          139

2.0 Planning Process Group: OT operational technology   141

2.1 Project Management Plan: OT operational technology
143

2.2 Scope Management Plan: OT operational technology 145

2.3 Requirements Management Plan: OT operational
technology   147

2.4 Requirements Documentation: OT operational
technology   149

2.5 Requirements Traceability Matrix: OT operational
technology   151

2.6 Project Scope Statement: OT operational technology 153

2.7 Assumption and Constraint Log: OT operational
technology   155

2.8 Work Breakdown Structure: OT operational technology
157

2.9 WBS Dictionary: OT operational technology   159

2.10 Schedule Management Plan: OT operational
technology   161

2.11 Activity List: OT operational technology   163

2.12 Activity Attributes: OT operational technology   165

2.13 Milestone List: OT operational technology   167

2.14 Network Diagram: OT operational technology   169

2.15 Activity Resource Requirements: OT operational
technology   171

2.16 Resource Breakdown Structure: OT operational technology   173

2.17 Activity Duration Estimates: OT operational technology   175

2.18 Duration Estimating Worksheet: OT operational technology   177

2.19 Project Schedule: OT operational technology   179

2.20 Cost Management Plan: OT operational technology 181

2.21 Activity Cost Estimates: OT operational technology   183

2.22 Cost Estimating Worksheet: OT operational technology   185

2.23 Cost Baseline: OT operational technology   187

2.24 Quality Management Plan: OT operational technology   189

2.25 Quality Metrics: OT operational technology   191

2.26 Process Improvement Plan: OT operational technology   193

2.27 Responsibility Assignment Matrix: OT operational technology   195

2.28 Roles and Responsibilities: OT operational technology   197

2.29 Human Resource Management Plan: OT operational technology   199

2.30 Communications Management Plan: OT operational technology 201

2.31 Risk Management Plan: OT operational technology 203

2.32 Risk Register: OT operational technology 205

2.33 Probability and Impact Assessment: OT operational technology 207

2.34 Probability and Impact Matrix: OT operational technology 209

2.35 Risk Data Sheet: OT operational technology 211

2.36 Procurement Management Plan: OT operational technology 213

2.37 Source Selection Criteria: OT operational technology 215

2.38 Stakeholder Management Plan: OT operational technology 217

2.39 Change Management Plan: OT operational technology 219

3.0 Executing Process Group: OT operational technology 221

3.1 Team Member Status Report: OT operational technology 223

3.2 Change Request: OT operational technology 225

3.3 Change Log: OT operational technology 227

3.4 Decision Log: OT operational technology 229

3.5 Quality Audit: OT operational technology   231

3.6 Team Directory: OT operational technology   234

3.7 Team Operating Agreement: OT operational technology
    236

3.8 Team Performance Assessment: OT operational
technology   238

3.9 Team Member Performance Assessment: OT operational
technology   240

3.10 Issue Log: OT operational technology   242

4.0 Monitoring and Controlling Process Group: OT
operational technology   244

4.1 Project Performance Report: OT operational technology
    246

4.2 Variance Analysis: OT operational technology   248

4.3 Earned Value Status: OT operational technology   250

4.4 Risk Audit: OT operational technology   252

4.5 Contractor Status Report: OT operational technology 254

4.6 Formal Acceptance: OT operational technology   256

5.0 Closing Process Group: OT operational technology   258

5.1 Procurement Audit: OT operational technology   260

5.2 Contract Close-Out: OT operational technology   263

5.3 Project or Phase Close-Out: OT operational technology
265

5.4 Lessons Learned: OT operational technology   267
Index   269

About The Art of Service

The Art of Service, Business Process Architects since 2000, is dedicated to helping stakeholders achieve excellence.

Defining, designing, creating, and implementing a process to solve a stakeholders challenge or meet an objective is the most valuable role… In EVERY group, company, organization and department.

Unless you're talking a one-time, single-use project, there should be a process. Whether that process is managed and implemented by humans, AI, or a combination of the two, it needs to be designed by someone with a complex enough perspective to ask the right questions.

Someone capable of asking the right questions and step back and say, 'What are we really trying to accomplish here? And is there a different way to look at it?'

With The Art of Service's Self-Assessments, we empower people who can do just that — whether their title is marketer, entrepreneur, manager, salesperson, consultant, Business Process Manager, executive assistant, IT Manager, CIO etc... —they are the people who rule the future. They are people who watch the process as it happens, and ask the right questions to make the process work better.

Contact us when you need any support with this Self-Assessment and any help with templates, blue-prints and examples of standard documents you might need:

https://theartofservice.com
support@theartofservice.com

Included Resources - how to access

Included with your purchase of the book is the OT operational

technology Self-Assessment Spreadsheet Dashboard which contains all questions and Self-Assessment areas and auto-generates insights, graphs, and project RACI planning - all with examples to get you started right away.

How? Simply send an email to **access@theartofservice.com** with this books' title in the subject to get the OT operational technology Self Assessment Tool right away.

The auto reply will guide you further, you will then receive the following contents with New and Updated specific criteria:

- The latest quick edition of the book in PDF

- The latest complete edition of the book in PDF, which criteria correspond to the criteria in...

- The Self-Assessment Excel Dashboard, and...

- Example pre-filled Self-Assessment Excel Dashboard to get familiar with results generation

- In-depth specific Checklists covering the topic

- Project management checklists and templates to assist with implementation

INCLUDES LIFETIME SELF ASSESSMENT UPDATES

Every self assessment comes with Lifetime Updates and Lifetime Free Updated Books. Lifetime Updates is an industry-first feature which allows you to receive verified self assessment updates, ensuring you always have the most accurate information at your fingertips.

Get it now- you will be glad you did - do it now, before you forget.

Send an email to **access@theartofservice.com** with this books' title in the subject to get the OT operational technology Self Assessment Tool right away.

Purpose of this Self-Assessment

This Self-Assessment has been developed to improve understanding of the requirements and elements of OT operational technology, based on best practices and standards in business process architecture, design and quality management.

It is designed to allow for a rapid Self-Assessment to determine how closely existing management practices and procedures correspond to the elements of the Self-Assessment.

The criteria of requirements and elements of OT operational technology have been rephrased in the format of a Self-Assessment questionnaire, with a seven-criterion scoring system, as explained in this document.

In this format, even with limited background knowledge of OT operational technology, a manager can quickly review existing operations to determine how they measure up to the standards. This in turn can serve as the starting point of a 'gap analysis' to identify management tools or system elements that might usefully be implemented in the organization to help improve overall performance.

How to use the Self-Assessment

On the following pages are a series of questions to identify to what extent your OT operational technology initiative is complete in comparison to the requirements set in standards.

To facilitate answering the questions, there is a space in front of each question to enter a score on a scale of '1' to '5'.

> 1 Strongly Disagree
>
> 2 Disagree
>
> 3 Neutral
>
> 4 Agree
>
> 5 Strongly Agree

Read the question and rate it with the following in front of mind:

'In my belief, the answer to this question is clearly defined'.

There are two ways in which you can choose to interpret this statement;
1. how aware are you that the answer to the question is clearly defined
2. for more in-depth analysis you can choose to gather evidence and confirm the answer to the question. This obviously will take more time, most Self-Assessment users opt for the first way to interpret the question and dig deeper later on based on the outcome of the overall Self-Assessment.

A score of '1' would mean that the answer is not clear at all, where a '5' would mean the answer is crystal clear and defined. Leave emtpy when the question is not applicable or you don't want to answer it, you can skip it without affecting your score. Write your score in the space provided.

After you have responded to all the appropriate statements in each section, compute your average score for that section, using the formula provided, and round to the nearest tenth. Then transfer to the corresponding spoke in the OT operational technology Scorecard on the second next page of the Self-Assessment.

Your completed OT operational technology Scorecard will give you a clear presentation of which OT operational technology areas need attention.

OT operational technology Scorecard Example

Example of how the finalized Scorecard can look like:

OT operational technology Scorecard

Your Scores:

BEGINNING OF THE SELF-ASSESSMENT:

CRITERION #1: RECOGNIZE

INTENT: Be aware of the need for change. Recognize that there is an unfavorable variation, problem or symptom.

In my belief, the answer to this question is clearly defined:

5 Strongly Agree

4 Agree

3 Neutral

2 Disagree

1 Strongly Disagree

1. What is the OT operational technology problem definition? What do you need to resolve?
<--- Score

2. Can management personnel recognize the monetary benefit of OT operational technology?
<--- Score

3. What OT operational technology coordination do

you need?
<--- Score

4. Do you need to avoid or amend any OT operational technology activities?
<--- Score

5. How do you assess your OT operational technology workforce capability and capacity needs, including skills, competencies, and staffing levels?
<--- Score

6. Why the need?
<--- Score

7. Are employees recognized or rewarded for performance that demonstrates the highest levels of integrity?
<--- Score

8. What are the minority interests and what amount of minority interests can be recognized?
<--- Score

9. To what extent does each concerned units management team recognize OT operational technology as an effective investment?
<--- Score

10. How do you recognize an OT operational technology objection?
<--- Score

11. Is the need for organizational change recognized?
<--- Score

12. Which issues are too important to ignore?
<--- Score

13. Which needs are not included or involved?
<--- Score

14. Looking at each person individually – does every one have the qualities which are needed to work in this group?
<--- Score

15. Are there regulatory / compliance issues?
<--- Score

16. Why is this needed?
<--- Score

17. How are training requirements identified?
<--- Score

18. Who else hopes to benefit from it?
<--- Score

19. How are the OT operational technology's objectives aligned to the group's overall stakeholder strategy?
<--- Score

20. Who are your key stakeholders who need to sign off?
<--- Score

21. What information do users need?
<--- Score

22. Do you recognize OT operational technology

achievements?
<--- Score

23. What prevents you from making the changes you know will make you a more effective OT operational technology leader?
<--- Score

24. Are your goals realistic? Do you need to redefine your problem? Perhaps the problem has changed or maybe you have reached your goal and need to set a new one?
<--- Score

25. Is it needed?
<--- Score

26. Will a response program recognize when a crisis occurs and provide some level of response?
<--- Score

27. How are you going to measure success?
<--- Score

28. Will new equipment/products be required to facilitate OT operational technology delivery, for example is new software needed?
<--- Score

29. Where is training needed?
<--- Score

30. Does the problem have ethical dimensions?
<--- Score

31. What resources or support might you need?

<--- Score

32. What vendors make products that address the OT operational technology needs?
<--- Score

33. Who needs to know about OT operational technology?
<--- Score

34. Think about the people you identified for your OT operational technology project and the project responsibilities you would assign to them, what kind of training do you think they would need to perform these responsibilities effectively?
<--- Score

35. Are problem definition and motivation clearly presented?
<--- Score

36. Who should resolve the OT operational technology issues?
<--- Score

37. How does it fit into your organizational needs and tasks?
<--- Score

38. Are there recognized OT operational technology problems?
<--- Score

39. What training and capacity building actions are needed to implement proposed reforms?
<--- Score

40. How much are sponsors, customers, partners, stakeholders involved in OT operational technology? In other words, what are the risks, if OT operational technology does not deliver successfully?
<--- Score

41. What do you need to start doing?
<--- Score

42. Whom do you really need or want to serve?
<--- Score

43. What do employees need in the short term?
<--- Score

44. Are losses recognized in a timely manner?
<--- Score

45. What should be considered when identifying available resources, constraints, and deadlines?
<--- Score

46. What tools and technologies are needed for a custom OT operational technology project?
<--- Score

47. What are the OT operational technology resources needed?
<--- Score

48. Are controls defined to recognize and contain problems?
<--- Score

49. What situation(s) led to this OT operational

technology Self Assessment?

<--- Score

50. What OT operational technology events should you attend?

<--- Score

51. Will it solve real problems?

<--- Score

52. Does OT operational technology create potential expectations in other areas that need to be recognized and considered?

<--- Score

53. What would happen if OT operational technology weren't done?

<--- Score

54. Do you know what you need to know about OT operational technology?

<--- Score

55. Are there any specific expectations or concerns about the OT operational technology team, OT operational technology itself?

<--- Score

56. Have you identified your OT operational technology key performance indicators?

<--- Score

57. For your OT operational technology project, identify and describe the business environment, is there more than one layer to the business environment?

<--- Score

58. What activities does the governance board need to consider?
<--- Score

59. What OT operational technology problem should be solved?
<--- Score

60. What is the recognized need?
<--- Score

61. Did you miss any major OT operational technology issues?
<--- Score

62. What are the stakeholder objectives to be achieved with OT operational technology?
<--- Score

63. What does OT operational technology success mean to the stakeholders?
<--- Score

64. Are there OT operational technology problems defined?
<--- Score

65. Would you recognize a threat from the inside?
<--- Score

66. Will OT operational technology deliverables need to be tested and, if so, by whom?
<--- Score

67. How do you identify subcontractor relationships?
<--- Score

68. Are you dealing with any of the same issues today as yesterday? What can you do about this?
<--- Score

69. What are the timeframes required to resolve each of the issues/problems?
<--- Score

70. Where do you need to exercise leadership?
<--- Score

71. Who needs budgets?
<--- Score

72. Who needs what information?
<--- Score

73. How many trainings, in total, are needed?
<--- Score

74. What OT operational technology capabilities do you need?
<--- Score

75. How do you take a forward-looking perspective in identifying OT operational technology research related to market response and models?
<--- Score

76. What is the problem or issue?
<--- Score

77. Is it clear when you think of the day ahead of you

what activities and tasks you need to complete?
<--- Score

78. What is the smallest subset of the problem you can usefully solve?
<--- Score

79. Do you need different information or graphics?
<--- Score

80. What extra resources will you need?
<--- Score

81. Consider your own OT operational technology project, what types of organizational problems do you think might be causing or affecting your problem, based on the work done so far?
<--- Score

82. What problems are you facing and how do you consider OT operational technology will circumvent those obstacles?
<--- Score

83. How can auditing be a preventative security measure?
<--- Score

84. To what extent would your organization benefit from being recognized as a award recipient?
<--- Score

85. What are your needs in relation to OT operational technology skills, labor, equipment, and markets?
<--- Score

86. What is the problem and/or vulnerability?
<--- Score

87. Are employees recognized for desired behaviors?
<--- Score

88. When a OT operational technology manager recognizes a problem, what options are available?
<--- Score

89. Is the quality assurance team identified?
<--- Score

90. Who defines the rules in relation to any given issue?
<--- Score

91. As a sponsor, customer or management, how important is it to meet goals, objectives?
<--- Score

92. What are the expected benefits of OT operational technology to the stakeholder?
<--- Score

93. What needs to stay?
<--- Score

94. What else needs to be measured?
<--- Score

95. Which information does the OT operational technology business case need to include?
<--- Score

96. Do you have/need 24-hour access to key

personnel?
<--- Score

97. What creative shifts do you need to take?
<--- Score

98. What needs to be done?
<--- Score

Add up total points for this section:
_ _ _ _ _ = Total points for this section

Divided by: _ _ _ _ _ _ (number of
statements answered) = _ _ _ _ _ _
Average score for this section

Transfer your score to the OT
operational technology Index at the
beginning of the Self-Assessment.

CRITERION #2: DEFINE:

INTENT: Formulate the stakeholder problem. Define the problem, needs and objectives.

In my belief, the answer to this question is clearly defined:

5 Strongly Agree

4 Agree

3 Neutral

2 Disagree

1 Strongly Disagree

1. Is OT operational technology currently on schedule according to the plan?
<--- Score

2. Are there any constraints known that bear on the ability to perform OT operational technology work? How is the team addressing them?
<--- Score

3. How and when will the baselines be defined?
<--- Score

4. Are approval levels defined for contracts and supplements to contracts?
<--- Score

5. What are the OT operational technology tasks and definitions?
<--- Score

6. Is OT operational technology linked to key stakeholder goals and objectives?
<--- Score

7. Is the team adequately staffed with the desired cross-functionality? If not, what additional resources are available to the team?
<--- Score

8. If substitutes have been appointed, have they been briefed on the OT operational technology goals and received regular communications as to the progress to date?
<--- Score

9. Who defines (or who defined) the rules and roles?
<--- Score

10. What are the Roles and Responsibilities for each team member and its leadership? Where is this documented?
<--- Score

11. Are the OT operational technology requirements complete?

<--- Score

12. Does the scope remain the same?
<--- Score

13. What are the core elements of the OT operational technology business case?
<--- Score

14. Are the OT operational technology requirements testable?
<--- Score

15. What sources do you use to gather information for a OT operational technology study?
<--- Score

16. How do you gather the stories?
<--- Score

17. What would be the goal or target for a OT operational technology's improvement team?
<--- Score

18. Is there a completed SIPOC representation, describing the Suppliers, Inputs, Process, Outputs, and Customers?
<--- Score

19. How did the OT operational technology manager receive input to the development of a OT operational technology improvement plan and the estimated completion dates/times of each activity?
<--- Score

20. Is there a OT operational technology management

charter, including stakeholder case, problem and goal statements, scope, milestones, roles and responsibilities, communication plan?
<--- Score

21. When is the estimated completion date?
<--- Score

22. Are required metrics defined, what are they?
<--- Score

23. Is the OT operational technology scope manageable?
<--- Score

24. When are meeting minutes sent out? Who is on the distribution list?
<--- Score

25. Do the problem and goal statements meet the SMART criteria (specific, measurable, attainable, relevant, and time-bound)?
<--- Score

26. Is it clearly defined in and to your organization what you do?
<--- Score

27. Are accountability and ownership for OT operational technology clearly defined?
<--- Score

28. Has a OT operational technology requirement not been met?
<--- Score

29. Have all of the relationships been defined properly?
<--- Score

30. What are the requirements for audit information?
<--- Score

31. How will variation in the actual durations of each activity be dealt with to ensure that the expected OT operational technology results are met?
<--- Score

32. What is the scope?
<--- Score

33. Will team members regularly document their OT operational technology work?
<--- Score

34. Is the current 'as is' process being followed? If not, what are the discrepancies?
<--- Score

35. What is the scope of the OT operational technology effort?
<--- Score

36. What knowledge or experience is required?
<--- Score

37. Who is gathering OT operational technology information?
<--- Score

38. What customer feedback methods were used to solicit their input?

<--- Score

39. How have you defined all OT operational technology requirements first?
<--- Score

40. What is the definition of success?
<--- Score

41. What is the definition of OT operational technology excellence?
<--- Score

42. Has/have the customer(s) been identified?
<--- Score

43. Have the customer needs been translated into specific, measurable requirements? How?
<--- Score

44. Are different versions of process maps needed to account for the different types of inputs?
<--- Score

45. Is there a completed, verified, and validated high-level 'as is' (not 'should be' or 'could be') stakeholder process map?
<--- Score

46. Is there a critical path to deliver OT operational technology results?
<--- Score

47. What are the OT operational technology use cases?
<--- Score

48. What are the rough order estimates on cost savings/opportunities that OT operational technology brings?
<--- Score

49. How would you define the culture at your organization, how susceptible is it to OT operational technology changes?
<--- Score

50. What are the tasks and definitions?
<--- Score

51. What are (control) requirements for OT operational technology Information?
<--- Score

52. What information do you gather?
<--- Score

53. How do you catch OT operational technology definition inconsistencies?
<--- Score

54. Has the OT operational technology work been fairly and/or equitably divided and delegated among team members who are qualified and capable to perform the work? Has everyone contributed?
<--- Score

55. What constraints exist that might impact the team?
<--- Score

56. What scope do you want your strategy to cover?

<--- Score

57. Will a OT operational technology production readiness review be required?
<--- Score

58. What is out-of-scope initially?
<--- Score

59. When is/was the OT operational technology start date?
<--- Score

60. Are there different segments of customers?
<--- Score

61. Has anyone else (internal or external to the group) attempted to solve this problem or a similar one before? If so, what knowledge can be leveraged from these previous efforts?
<--- Score

62. Is data collected and displayed to better understand customer(s) critical needs and requirements.
<--- Score

63. Does the team have regular meetings?
<--- Score

64. How do you think the partners involved in OT operational technology would have defined success?
<--- Score

65. Is the OT operational technology scope complete and appropriately sized?

<--- Score

66. Is the scope of OT operational technology defined?
<--- Score

67. Is there any additional OT operational technology definition of success?
<--- Score

68. What are the boundaries of the scope? What is in bounds and what is not? What is the start point? What is the stop point?
<--- Score

69. What sort of initial information to gather?
<--- Score

70. In what way can you redefine the criteria of choice clients have in your category in your favor?
<--- Score

71. Do you have organizational privacy requirements?
<--- Score

72. Who is gathering information?
<--- Score

73. Are task requirements clearly defined?
<--- Score

74. What was the context?
<--- Score

75. How do you manage scope?
<--- Score

76. Is there regularly 100% attendance at the team meetings? If not, have appointed substitutes attended to preserve cross-functionality and full representation?
<--- Score

77. How do you keep key subject matter experts in the loop?
<--- Score

78. Are customer(s) identified and segmented according to their different needs and requirements?
<--- Score

79. What defines best in class?
<--- Score

80. Has everyone on the team, including the team leaders, been properly trained?
<--- Score

81. How is the team tracking and documenting its work?
<--- Score

82. What is the worst case scenario?
<--- Score

83. What is the context?
<--- Score

84. What are the record-keeping requirements of OT operational technology activities?
<--- Score

85. Who are the OT operational technology improvement team members, including Management Leads and Coaches?
<--- Score

86. How often are the team meetings?
<--- Score

87. How do you gather requirements?
<--- Score

88. Has a high-level 'as is' process map been completed, verified and validated?
<--- Score

89. Has the improvement team collected the 'voice of the customer' (obtained feedback – qualitative and quantitative)?
<--- Score

90. How does the OT operational technology manager ensure against scope creep?
<--- Score

91. Is the team equipped with available and reliable resources?
<--- Score

92. Are all requirements met?
<--- Score

93. What OT operational technology requirements should be gathered?
<--- Score

94. How can the value of OT operational technology

be defined?
<--- Score

95. What information should you gather?
<--- Score

96. What is in the scope and what is not in scope?
<--- Score

97. What gets examined?
<--- Score

98. Are resources adequate for the scope?
<--- Score

99. What specifically is the problem? Where does it occur? When does it occur? What is its extent?
<--- Score

100. Are audit criteria, scope, frequency and methods defined?
<--- Score

101. Is the improvement team aware of the different versions of a process: what they think it is vs. what it actually is vs. what it should be vs. what it could be?
<--- Score

102. Is scope creep really all bad news?
<--- Score

103. How are consistent OT operational technology definitions important?
<--- Score

104. The political context: who holds power?

<--- Score

105. Is OT operational technology required?
<--- Score

106. What baselines are required to be defined and managed?
<--- Score

107. What is out of scope?
<--- Score

108. How was the 'as is' process map developed, reviewed, verified and validated?
<--- Score

109. What are the compelling stakeholder reasons for embarking on OT operational technology?
<--- Score

110. How do you hand over OT operational technology context?
<--- Score

111. Have specific policy objectives been defined?
<--- Score

112. Is the work to date meeting requirements?
<--- Score

113. What is in scope?
<--- Score

114. What system do you use for gathering OT operational technology information?
<--- Score

115. What scope to assess?
<--- Score

116. How do you gather OT operational technology requirements?
<--- Score

117. Where can you gather more information?
<--- Score

118. How will the OT operational technology team and the group measure complete success of OT operational technology?
<--- Score

119. Scope of sensitive information?
<--- Score

120. Is special OT operational technology user knowledge required?
<--- Score

121. What key stakeholder process output measure(s) does OT operational technology leverage and how?
<--- Score

122. What are the dynamics of the communication plan?
<--- Score

123. Has a team charter been developed and communicated?
<--- Score

124. Has a project plan, Gantt chart, or similar been

developed/completed?
<--- Score

125. Who approved the OT operational technology scope?
<--- Score

126. Has the direction changed at all during the course of OT operational technology? If so, when did it change and why?
<--- Score

127. Do you all define OT operational technology in the same way?
<--- Score

128. Is there a clear OT operational technology case definition?
<--- Score

129. How do you build the right business case?
<--- Score

130. What is the scope of the OT operational technology work?
<--- Score

131. Why are you doing OT operational technology and what is the scope?
<--- Score

132. Has your scope been defined?
<--- Score

133. What critical content must be communicated – who, what, when, where, and how?

<--- Score

134. How do you manage unclear OT operational technology requirements?
<--- Score

135. What is a worst-case scenario for losses?
<--- Score

136. How do you manage changes in OT operational technology requirements?
<--- Score

137. How would you define OT operational technology leadership?
<--- Score

138. What happens if OT operational technology's scope changes?
<--- Score

139. What intelligence can you gather?
<--- Score

140. Are roles and responsibilities formally defined?
<--- Score

141. Have all basic functions of OT operational technology been defined?
<--- Score

Add up total points for this section:
_ _ _ _ _ = Total points for this section

Divided by: _ _ _ _ _ _ (number of statements answered) = _ _ _ _ _ _

Average score for this section

Transfer your score to the OT
operational technology Index at the
beginning of the Self-Assessment.

CRITERION #3: MEASURE:

INTENT: Gather the correct data. Measure the current performance and evolution of the situation.

In my belief, the answer to this question is clearly defined:

5 Strongly Agree

4 Agree

3 Neutral

2 Disagree

1 Strongly Disagree

1. The approach of traditional OT operational technology works for detail complexity but is focused on a systematic approach rather than an understanding of the nature of systems themselves, what approach will permit your organization to deal with the kind of unpredictable emergent behaviors that dynamic complexity can introduce?
<--- Score

2. What are the uncertainties surrounding estimates of impact?
<--- Score

3. What are the costs and benefits?
<--- Score

4. What could cause delays in the schedule?
<--- Score

5. What does your operating model cost?
<--- Score

6. What is an unallowable cost?
<--- Score

7. How can you measure the performance?
<--- Score

8. Where is the cost?
<--- Score

9. Are the measurements objective?
<--- Score

10. Have you included everything in your OT operational technology cost models?
<--- Score

11. What is the cause of any OT operational technology gaps?
<--- Score

12. Do you effectively measure and reward individual and team performance?
<--- Score

13. What are the types and number of measures to use?
<--- Score

14. How will effects be measured?
<--- Score

15. What happens if cost savings do not materialize?
<--- Score

16. What tests verify requirements?
<--- Score

17. Are supply costs steady or fluctuating?
<--- Score

18. How do you measure variability?
<--- Score

19. How do you focus on what is right -not who is right?
<--- Score

20. When are costs are incurred?
<--- Score

21. Are OT operational technology vulnerabilities categorized and prioritized?
<--- Score

22. How are you verifying it?
<--- Score

23. What is your decision requirements diagram?
<--- Score

24. What would be a real cause for concern?
<--- Score

25. How will measures be used to manage and adapt?
<--- Score

26. What do people want to verify?
<--- Score

27. What are you verifying?
<--- Score

28. How are costs allocated?
<--- Score

29. What causes mismanagement?
<--- Score

30. What measurements are possible, practicable and meaningful?
<--- Score

31. How will you measure success?
<--- Score

32. What causes innovation to fail or succeed in your organization?
<--- Score

33. How do you verify the authenticity of the data and information used?
<--- Score

34. How are measurements made?
<--- Score

35. What users will be impacted?
<--- Score

36. Do you have any cost OT operational technology limitation requirements?
<--- Score

37. What evidence is there and what is measured?
<--- Score

38. Do you have a flow diagram of what happens?
<--- Score

39. What potential environmental factors impact the OT operational technology effort?
<--- Score

40. How do you verify performance?
<--- Score

41. Have you made assumptions about the shape of the future, particularly its impact on your customers and competitors?
<--- Score

42. What are the current costs of the OT operational technology process?
<--- Score

43. What causes investor action?
<--- Score

44. How is progress measured?
<--- Score

45. How will success or failure be measured?
<--- Score

46. Who should receive measurement reports?
<--- Score

47. Where can you go to verify the info?
<--- Score

48. What are your key OT operational technology organizational performance measures, including key short and longer-term financial measures?
<--- Score

49. How do you verify and develop ideas and innovations?
<--- Score

50. How is performance measured?
<--- Score

51. How will your organization measure success?
<--- Score

52. What is the root cause(s) of the problem?
<--- Score

53. How do your measurements capture actionable OT operational technology information for use in exceeding your customers expectations and securing your customers engagement?
<--- Score

54. What is your OT operational technology quality cost segregation study?
<--- Score

55. How do you prevent mis-estimating cost?
<--- Score

56. What details are required of the OT operational technology cost structure?
<--- Score

57. How do you verify your resources?
<--- Score

58. Are actual costs in line with budgeted costs?
<--- Score

59. Is there an opportunity to verify requirements?
<--- Score

60. Which costs should be taken into account?
<--- Score

61. What drives O&M cost?
<--- Score

62. How can a OT operational technology test verify your ideas or assumptions?
<--- Score

63. How do you control the overall costs of your work processes?
<--- Score

64. What are allowable costs?
<--- Score

65. What could cause you to change course?
<--- Score

66. Are you able to realize any cost savings?
<--- Score

67. Among the OT operational technology product and service cost to be estimated, which is considered hardest to estimate?
<--- Score

68. What are the strategic priorities for this year?
<--- Score

69. Are there any easy-to-implement alternatives to OT operational technology? Sometimes other solutions are available that do not require the cost implications of a full-blown project?
<--- Score

70. Are you aware of what could cause a problem?
<--- Score

71. What are your operating costs?
<--- Score

72. How frequently do you verify your OT operational technology strategy?
<--- Score

73. What are the OT operational technology key cost drivers?
<--- Score

74. Who pays the cost?
<--- Score

75. What is the OT operational technology business

impact?

<--- Score

76. How do you verify if OT operational technology is built right?

<--- Score

77. What are your customers expectations and measures?

<--- Score

78. Are there competing OT operational technology priorities?

<--- Score

79. When should you bother with diagrams?

<--- Score

80. How do you measure lifecycle phases?

<--- Score

81. Is the cost worth the OT operational technology effort ?

<--- Score

82. Are the units of measure consistent?

<--- Score

83. How do you measure efficient delivery of OT operational technology services?

<--- Score

84. How frequently do you track OT operational technology measures?

<--- Score

85. Who is involved in verifying compliance?
<--- Score

86. Are missed OT operational technology opportunities costing your organization money?
<--- Score

87. How do you measure success?
<--- Score

88. How do you stay flexible and focused to recognize larger OT operational technology results?
<--- Score

89. Where is it measured?
<--- Score

90. How do you quantify and qualify impacts?
<--- Score

91. Which measures and indicators matter?
<--- Score

92. What is measured? Why?
<--- Score

93. How can you manage cost down?
<--- Score

94. What do you measure and why?
<--- Score

95. How much does it cost?
<--- Score

96. How can you measure OT operational technology

in a systematic way?
<--- Score

97. Did you tackle the cause or the symptom?
<--- Score

98. Why a OT operational technology focus?
<--- Score

99. What causes extra work or rework?
<--- Score

100. Does management have the right priorities among projects?
<--- Score

101. What are the operational costs after OT operational technology deployment?
<--- Score

102. What can be used to verify compliance?
<--- Score

103. How will you measure your OT operational technology effectiveness?
<--- Score

104. How do you verify and validate the OT operational technology data?
<--- Score

105. Do the benefits outweigh the costs?
<--- Score

106. What are the estimated costs of proposed changes?

<--- Score

107. Are you taking your company in the direction of better and revenue or cheaper and cost?
<--- Score

108. How do you verify the OT operational technology requirements quality?
<--- Score

109. Are indirect costs charged to the OT operational technology program?
<--- Score

110. Do you verify that corrective actions were taken?
<--- Score

111. When a disaster occurs, who gets priority?
<--- Score

112. How do you aggregate measures across priorities?
<--- Score

113. What is the total fixed cost?
<--- Score

114. What harm might be caused?
<--- Score

115. What are the costs of delaying OT operational technology action?
<--- Score

116. Are there measurements based on task performance?

<--- Score

117. What does verifying compliance entail?
<--- Score

118. Are the OT operational technology benefits worth its costs?
<--- Score

119. What methods are feasible and acceptable to estimate the impact of reforms?
<--- Score

120. How sensitive must the OT operational technology strategy be to cost?
<--- Score

121. What disadvantage does this cause for the user?
<--- Score

122. Is the solution cost-effective?
<--- Score

123. What are the costs?
<--- Score

124. How will costs be allocated?
<--- Score

125. What are your primary costs, revenues, assets?
<--- Score

126. What relevant entities could be measured?
<--- Score

127. Was a business case (cost/benefit) developed?

<--- Score

128. How do you verify OT operational technology completeness and accuracy?
<--- Score

129. What measurements are being captured?
<--- Score

130. Is a follow-up focused external OT operational technology review required?
<--- Score

131. What does a Test Case verify?
<--- Score

132. Has a cost center been established?
<--- Score

133. What would it cost to replace your technology?
<--- Score

134. How long to keep data and how to manage retention costs?
<--- Score

135. Does a OT operational technology quantification method exist?
<--- Score

Add up total points for this section:
_ _ _ _ _ = Total points for this section

Divided by: _ _ _ _ _ _ (number of statements answered) = _ _ _ _ _ _
Average score for this section

Transfer your score to the OT
operational technology Index at the
beginning of the Self-Assessment.

CRITERION #4: ANALYZE:

INTENT: Analyze causes, assumptions and hypotheses.

In my belief, the answer to this question is clearly defined:

5 Strongly Agree

4 Agree

3 Neutral

2 Disagree

1 Strongly Disagree

1. Do you take regular backups of your systems and data?
<--- Score

2. Where is the data coming from to measure compliance?
<--- Score

3. Who will gather what data?
<--- Score

4. Is the final output clearly identified?
<--- Score

5. How is the way you as the leader think and process information affecting your organizational culture?
<--- Score

6. What are your current levels and trends in key OT operational technology measures or indicators of product and process performance that are important to and directly serve your customers?
<--- Score

7. What methods do you use to gather OT operational technology data?
<--- Score

8. What is the cost of poor quality as supported by the team's analysis?
<--- Score

9. What, related to, OT operational technology processes does your organization outsource?
<--- Score

10. How has the OT operational technology data been gathered?
<--- Score

11. How will the data be checked for quality?
<--- Score

12. Should you invest in industry-recognized qualifications?
<--- Score

13. Is data and process analysis, root cause analysis and quantifying the gap/opportunity in place?
<--- Score

14. What is your organizations process which leads to recognition of value generation?
<--- Score

15. What conclusions were drawn from the team's data collection and analysis? How did the team reach these conclusions?
<--- Score

16. Do several people in different organizational units assist with the OT operational technology process?
<--- Score

17. What are your OT operational technology processes?
<--- Score

18. What data is gathered?
<--- Score

19. Where can you get qualified talent today?
<--- Score

20. What are your key performance measures or indicators and in-process measures for the control and improvement of your OT operational technology processes?
<--- Score

21. Which OT operational technology data should be retained?

<--- Score

22. Are you missing OT operational technology opportunities?
<--- Score

23. Do you, as a leader, bounce back quickly from setbacks?
<--- Score

24. What qualifications are needed?
<--- Score

25. What other organizational variables, such as reward systems or communication systems, affect the performance of this OT operational technology process?
<--- Score

26. What did the team gain from developing a sub-process map?
<--- Score

27. Who gets your output?
<--- Score

28. Was a cause-and-effect diagram used to explore the different types of causes (or sources of variation)?
<--- Score

29. What are the OT operational technology design outputs?
<--- Score

30. What qualifies as competition?
<--- Score

31. How do you define collaboration and team output?
<--- Score

32. What other jobs or tasks affect the performance of the steps in the OT operational technology process?
<--- Score

33. A compounding model resolution with available relevant data can often provide insight towards a solution methodology; which OT operational technology models, tools and techniques are necessary?
<--- Score

34. What is the complexity of the output produced?
<--- Score

35. What are the personnel training and qualifications required?
<--- Score

36. What are your best practices for minimizing OT operational technology project risk, while demonstrating incremental value and quick wins throughout the OT operational technology project lifecycle?
<--- Score

37. Think about some of the processes you undertake within your organization, which do you own?
<--- Score

38. What types of data do your OT operational technology indicators require?

<--- Score

39. What OT operational technology data should be managed?
<--- Score

40. How will corresponding data be collected?
<--- Score

41. Who is involved with workflow mapping?
<--- Score

42. Identify an operational issue in your organization, for example, could a particular task be done more quickly or more efficiently by OT operational technology?
<--- Score

43. Have you defined which data is gathered how?
<--- Score

44. What controls do you have in place to protect data?
<--- Score

45. What were the crucial 'moments of truth' on the process map?
<--- Score

46. Is the performance gap determined?
<--- Score

47. How can risk management be tied procedurally to process elements?
<--- Score

48. How many input/output points does it require?
<--- Score

49. Do you have the authority to produce the output?
<--- Score

50. How do you use OT operational technology data and information to support organizational decision making and innovation?
<--- Score

51. What systems/processes must you excel at?
<--- Score

52. How do you identify specific OT operational technology investment opportunities and emerging trends?
<--- Score

53. How will the OT operational technology data be captured?
<--- Score

54. Were Pareto charts (or similar) used to portray the 'heavy hitters' (or key sources of variation)?
<--- Score

55. What are the necessary qualifications?
<--- Score

56. What qualifications and skills do you need?
<--- Score

57. Is there any way to speed up the process?
<--- Score

58. Where is OT operational technology data gathered?

<--- Score

59. What tools were used to generate the list of possible causes?

<--- Score

60. What are the best opportunities for value improvement?

<--- Score

61. What resources go in to get the desired output?

<--- Score

62. Are OT operational technology changes recognized early enough to be approved through the regular process?

<--- Score

63. Are your outputs consistent?

<--- Score

64. What do you need to qualify?

<--- Score

65. What are the disruptive OT operational technology technologies that enable your organization to radically change your business processes?

<--- Score

66. Is the gap/opportunity displayed and communicated in financial terms?

<--- Score

67. How is the data gathered?

<--- Score

68. What OT operational technology data will be collected?
<--- Score

69. What successful thing are you doing today that may be blinding you to new growth opportunities?
<--- Score

70. Do your employees have the opportunity to do what they do best everyday?
<--- Score

71. What is the output?
<--- Score

72. What are the processes for audit reporting and management?
<--- Score

73. An organizationally feasible system request is one that considers the mission, goals and objectives of the organization, key questions are: is the OT operational technology solution request practical and will it solve a problem or take advantage of an opportunity to achieve company goals?
<--- Score

74. Was a detailed process map created to amplify critical steps of the 'as is' stakeholder process?
<--- Score

75. Do quality systems drive continuous improvement?
<--- Score

76. Is the suppliers process defined and controlled?
<--- Score

77. What data do you need to collect?
<--- Score

78. What were the financial benefits resulting from any 'ground fruit or low-hanging fruit' (quick fixes)?
<--- Score

79. Do staff qualifications match your project?
<--- Score

80. What are your outputs?
<--- Score

81. How does the organization define, manage, and improve its OT operational technology processes?
<--- Score

82. How are outputs preserved and protected?
<--- Score

83. Are all staff in core OT operational technology subjects Highly Qualified?
<--- Score

84. Were any designed experiments used to generate additional insight into the data analysis?
<--- Score

85. Who is involved in the management review process?
<--- Score

86. How is the OT operational technology Value Stream Mapping managed?
<--- Score

87. How is data used for program management and improvement?
<--- Score

88. What does the data say about the performance of the stakeholder process?
<--- Score

89. Do your contracts/agreements contain data security obligations?
<--- Score

90. How do you measure the operational performance of your key work systems and processes, including productivity, cycle time, and other appropriate measures of process effectiveness, efficiency, and innovation?
<--- Score

91. What are the OT operational technology business drivers?
<--- Score

92. When should a process be art not science?
<--- Score

93. Is there a strict change management process?
<--- Score

94. What is the OT operational technology Driver?
<--- Score

95. Who owns what data?
<--- Score

96. Were there any improvement opportunities identified from the process analysis?
<--- Score

97. What quality tools were used to get through the analyze phase?
<--- Score

98. Are all team members qualified for all tasks?
<--- Score

99. How much data can be collected in the given timeframe?
<--- Score

100. Can you add value to the current OT operational technology decision-making process (largely qualitative) by incorporating uncertainty modeling (more quantitative)?
<--- Score

101. What tools were used to narrow the list of possible causes?
<--- Score

102. Do your leaders quickly bounce back from setbacks?
<--- Score

103. How will the change process be managed?
<--- Score

104. What training and qualifications will you need?

<--- Score

105. Is the required OT operational technology data gathered?
<--- Score

106. How do your work systems and key work processes relate to and capitalize on your core competencies?
<--- Score

107. What process should you select for improvement?
<--- Score

108. Is the OT operational technology process severely broken such that a re-design is necessary?
<--- Score

109. How often will data be collected for measures?
<--- Score

110. What information qualified as important?
<--- Score

111. What are the revised rough estimates of the financial savings/opportunity for OT operational technology improvements?
<--- Score

112. Is there an established change management process?
<--- Score

113. What process improvements will be needed?
<--- Score

114. What qualifications do OT operational technology leaders need?
<--- Score

115. How do mission and objectives affect the OT operational technology processes of your organization?
<--- Score

116. How was the detailed process map generated, verified, and validated?
<--- Score

117. Has data output been validated?
<--- Score

118. Who will facilitate the team and process?
<--- Score

119. What internal processes need improvement?
<--- Score

120. Think about the functions involved in your OT operational technology project, what processes flow from these functions?
<--- Score

121. What is the Value Stream Mapping?
<--- Score

122. What are evaluation criteria for the output?
<--- Score

123. What output to create?
<--- Score

124. What will drive OT operational technology change?
<--- Score

125. How is OT operational technology data gathered?
<--- Score

126. How do you implement and manage your work processes to ensure that they meet design requirements?
<--- Score

127. What qualifications are necessary?
<--- Score

128. How do you promote understanding that opportunity for improvement is not criticism of the status quo, or the people who created the status quo?
<--- Score

129. Do you understand your management processes today?
<--- Score

130. What OT operational technology data do you gather or use now?
<--- Score

131. What OT operational technology metrics are outputs of the process?
<--- Score

132. What is the oversight process?
<--- Score

133. Is pre-qualification of suppliers carried out?
<--- Score

134. Who qualifies to gain access to data?
<--- Score

135. Has an output goal been set?
<--- Score

Add up total points for this section:
_ _ _ _ _ = Total points for this section

Divided by: _ _ _ _ _ _ (number of
statements answered) = _ _ _ _ _ _
Average score for this section

Transfer your score to the OT
operational technology Index at the
beginning of the Self-Assessment.

CRITERION #5: IMPROVE:

INTENT: Develop a practical solution. Innovate, establish and test the solution and to measure the results.

In my belief, the answer to this question is clearly defined:

5 Strongly Agree

4 Agree

3 Neutral

2 Disagree

1 Strongly Disagree

1. How do you improve OT operational technology service perception, and satisfaction?
<--- Score

2. How do you define the solutions' scope?
<--- Score

3. Is a solution implementation plan established, including schedule/work breakdown structure,

resources, risk management plan, cost/budget, and control plan?
<--- Score

4. For decision problems, how do you develop a decision statement?
<--- Score

5. What were the underlying assumptions on the cost-benefit analysis?
<--- Score

6. What criteria will you use to assess your OT operational technology risks?
<--- Score

7. Who are the key stakeholders for the OT operational technology evaluation?
<--- Score

8. Do you cover the five essential competencies: Communication, Collaboration,Innovation, Adaptability, and Leadership that improve an organizations ability to leverage the new OT operational technology in a volatile global economy?
<--- Score

9. What went well, what should change, what can improve?
<--- Score

10. What is OT operational technology risk?
<--- Score

11. Is pilot data collected and analyzed?
<--- Score

12. Are events managed to resolution?
<--- Score

13. How will you recognize and celebrate results?
<--- Score

14. Who should make the OT operational technology decisions?
<--- Score

15. What needs improvement? Why?
<--- Score

16. Can you integrate quality management and risk management?
<--- Score

17. How do you improve productivity?
<--- Score

18. What tools were used to tap into the creativity and encourage 'outside the box' thinking?
<--- Score

19. How do you measure progress and evaluate training effectiveness?
<--- Score

20. What are the implications of the one critical OT operational technology decision 10 minutes, 10 months, and 10 years from now?
<--- Score

21. How can the phases of OT operational technology development be identified?

<--- Score

22. What are the expected OT operational technology results?
<--- Score

23. Is any OT operational technology documentation required?
<--- Score

24. Will the controls trigger any other risks?
<--- Score

25. Is there a small-scale pilot for proposed improvement(s)? What conclusions were drawn from the outcomes of a pilot?
<--- Score

26. What OT operational technology improvements can be made?
<--- Score

27. For estimation problems, how do you develop an estimation statement?
<--- Score

28. Are you assessing OT operational technology and risk?
<--- Score

29. Does a good decision guarantee a good outcome?
<--- Score

30. What were the criteria for evaluating a OT operational technology pilot?
<--- Score

31. How can you improve performance?
<--- Score

32. What are your current levels and trends in key measures or indicators of workforce and leader development?
<--- Score

33. Who will be responsible for making the decisions to include or exclude requested changes once OT operational technology is underway?
<--- Score

34. How are policy decisions made and where?
<--- Score

35. How can you better manage risk?
<--- Score

36. How do you link measurement and risk?
<--- Score

37. Is a contingency plan established?
<--- Score

38. Is there any other OT operational technology solution?
<--- Score

39. Were any criteria developed to assist the team in testing and evaluating potential solutions?
<--- Score

40. Who makes the OT operational technology decisions in your organization?

<--- Score

41. What should a proof of concept or pilot accomplish?
<--- Score

42. What is the implementation plan?
<--- Score

43. What attendant changes will need to be made to ensure that the solution is successful?
<--- Score

44. What strategies for OT operational technology improvement are successful?
<--- Score

45. Does the goal represent a desired result that can be measured?
<--- Score

46. Who are the people involved in developing and implementing OT operational technology?
<--- Score

47. Are procedures documented for managing OT operational technology risks?
<--- Score

48. What tools were used to evaluate the potential solutions?
<--- Score

49. What is the magnitude of the improvements?
<--- Score

50. Are decisions made in a timely manner?
<--- Score

51. Have you identified breakpoints and/or risk tolerances that will trigger broad consideration of a potential need for intervention or modification of strategy?
<--- Score

52. At what point will vulnerability assessments be performed once OT operational technology is put into production (e.g., ongoing Risk Management after implementation)?
<--- Score

53. What are the affordable OT operational technology risks?
<--- Score

54. Risk factors: what are the characteristics of OT operational technology that make it risky?
<--- Score

55. Is the implementation plan designed?
<--- Score

56. What tools were most useful during the improve phase?
<--- Score

57. Can the solution be designed and implemented within an acceptable time period?
<--- Score

58. Explorations of the frontiers of OT operational technology will help you build influence, improve OT

operational technology, optimize decision making, and sustain change, what is your approach?
<--- Score

59. How do you mitigate OT operational technology risk?
<--- Score

60. Are risk management tasks balanced centrally and locally?
<--- Score

61. Was a pilot designed for the proposed solution(s)?
<--- Score

62. Is the scope clearly documented?
<--- Score

63. Do vendor agreements bring new compliance risk ?
<--- Score

64. What is the team's contingency plan for potential problems occurring in implementation?
<--- Score

65. Is supporting OT operational technology documentation required?
<--- Score

66. What are the concrete OT operational technology results?
<--- Score

67. Who will be using the results of the measurement activities?

<--- Score

68. How will you know that you have improved?
<--- Score

69. Is OT operational technology documentation maintained?
<--- Score

70. What is the risk?
<--- Score

71. What error proofing will be done to address some of the discrepancies observed in the 'as is' process?
<--- Score

72. Is the optimal solution selected based on testing and analysis?
<--- Score

73. How are OT operational technology risks managed?
<--- Score

74. What actually has to improve and by how much?
<--- Score

75. What to do with the results or outcomes of measurements?
<--- Score

76. How do you deal with OT operational technology risk?
<--- Score

77. Would you develop a OT operational technology

Communication Strategy?
<--- Score

78. Who do you report OT operational technology results to?
<--- Score

79. Who controls key decisions that will be made?
<--- Score

80. What risks do you need to manage?
<--- Score

81. How can skill-level changes improve OT operational technology?
<--- Score

82. Was a OT operational technology charter developed?
<--- Score

83. How do you manage OT operational technology risk?
<--- Score

84. What area needs the greatest improvement?
<--- Score

85. Risk events: what are the things that could go wrong?
<--- Score

86. Is risk periodically assessed?
<--- Score

87. What can you do to improve?

<--- Score

88. What improvements have been achieved?
<--- Score

89. Do you need to do a usability evaluation?
<--- Score

90. How will you know that a change is an improvement?
<--- Score

91. Where do you need OT operational technology improvement?
<--- Score

92. How do you measure improved OT operational technology service perception, and satisfaction?
<--- Score

93. What practices helps your organization to develop its capacity to recognize patterns?
<--- Score

94. What is the OT operational technology's sustainability risk?
<--- Score

95. Risk Identification: What are the possible risk events your organization faces in relation to OT operational technology?
<--- Score

96. How do you manage and improve your OT operational technology work systems to deliver customer value and achieve organizational success

and sustainability?
<--- Score

97. How will you know when its improved?
<--- Score

98. Are the most efficient solutions problem-specific?
<--- Score

99. What are the OT operational technology security risks?
<--- Score

100. Who will be responsible for documenting the OT operational technology requirements in detail?
<--- Score

101. Is there a cost/benefit analysis of optimal solution(s)?
<--- Score

102. In the past few months, what is the smallest change you have made that has had the biggest positive result? What was it about that small change that produced the large return?
<--- Score

103. How do you improve your likelihood of success ?
<--- Score

104. If you could go back in time five years, what decision would you make differently? What is your best guess as to what decision you're making today you might regret five years from now?
<--- Score

105. Is the measure of success for OT operational technology understandable to a variety of people?
<--- Score

106. Where do the OT operational technology decisions reside?
<--- Score

107. Who manages OT operational technology risk?
<--- Score

108. OT operational technology risk decisions: whose call Is It?
<--- Score

109. How does your organization evaluate strategic OT operational technology success?
<--- Score

110. How significant is the improvement in the eyes of the end user?
<--- Score

111. When you map the key players in your own work and the types/domains of relationships with them, which relationships do you find easy and which challenging, and why?
<--- Score

112. Have you achieved OT operational technology improvements?
<--- Score

113. Who manages supplier risk management in your organization?
<--- Score

114. What tools do you use once you have decided on a OT operational technology strategy and more importantly how do you choose?
<--- Score

115. Are risk triggers captured?
<--- Score

116. What does the 'should be' process map/design look like?
<--- Score

117. How is continuous improvement applied to risk management?
<--- Score

118. What assumptions are made about the solution and approach?
<--- Score

119. Which of the recognised risks out of all risks can be most likely transferred?
<--- Score

120. Are the risks fully understood, reasonable and manageable?
<--- Score

121. How does the team improve its work?
<--- Score

122. Do those selected for the OT operational technology team have a good general understanding of what OT operational technology is all about?
<--- Score

123. What communications are necessary to support the implementation of the solution?
<--- Score

124. How do you keep improving OT operational technology?
<--- Score

125. How risky is your organization?
<--- Score

126. How scalable is your OT operational technology solution?
<--- Score

127. What lessons, if any, from a pilot were incorporated into the design of the full-scale solution?
<--- Score

128. Is there a high likelihood that any recommendations will achieve their intended results?
<--- Score

129. Is the OT operational technology documentation thorough?
<--- Score

130. How do you go about comparing OT operational technology approaches/solutions?
<--- Score

131. How do the OT operational technology results compare with the performance of your competitors and other organizations with similar offerings?
<--- Score

132. Are the key business and technology risks being managed?
<--- Score

133. What alternative responses are available to manage risk?
<--- Score

134. How will the team or the process owner(s) monitor the implementation plan to see that it is working as intended?
<--- Score

135. What resources are required for the improvement efforts?
<--- Score

136. What is OT operational technology's impact on utilizing the best solution(s)?
<--- Score

137. Who are the OT operational technology decision-makers?
<--- Score

138. Who are the OT operational technology decision makers?
<--- Score

139. Do you have the optimal project management team structure?
<--- Score

140. How do you decide how much to remunerate an employee?

<--- Score

141. Is the OT operational technology solution sustainable?
<--- Score

142. How is knowledge sharing about risk management improved?
<--- Score

Add up total points for this section:
_ _ _ _ _ = Total points for this section

Divided by: _ _ _ _ _ _ (number of statements answered) = _ _ _ _ _ _
Average score for this section

Transfer your score to the OT operational technology Index at the beginning of the Self-Assessment.

CRITERION #6: CONTROL:

INTENT: Implement the practical solution. Maintain the performance and correct possible complications.

In my belief, the answer to this question is clearly defined:

5 Strongly Agree

4 Agree

3 Neutral

2 Disagree

1 Strongly Disagree

1. How do you spread information?
<--- Score

2. What OT operational technology standards are applicable?
<--- Score

3. How do you encourage people to take control and responsibility?

<--- Score

4. Do you have a disaster recovery plan?
<--- Score

5. What are the key elements of your OT operational technology performance improvement system, including your evaluation, organizational learning, and innovation processes?
<--- Score

6. How might the group capture best practices and lessons learned so as to leverage improvements?
<--- Score

7. How do controls support value?
<--- Score

8. Is there a documented and implemented monitoring plan?
<--- Score

9. How do you monitor usage and cost?
<--- Score

10. Are there documented procedures?
<--- Score

11. Who will be in control?
<--- Score

12. What are you attempting to measure/monitor?
<--- Score

13. What key inputs and outputs are being measured on an ongoing basis?

<--- Score

14. Is there a recommended audit plan for routine surveillance inspections of OT operational technology's gains?
<--- Score

15. How will the day-to-day responsibilities for monitoring and continual improvement be transferred from the improvement team to the process owner?
<--- Score

16. How is OT operational technology project cost planned, managed, monitored?
<--- Score

17. Do the viable solutions scale to future needs?
<--- Score

18. What other systems, operations, processes, and infrastructures (hiring practices, staffing, training, incentives/rewards, metrics/dashboards/scorecards, etc.) need updates, additions, changes, or deletions in order to facilitate knowledge transfer and improvements?
<--- Score

19. Are you measuring, monitoring and predicting OT operational technology activities to optimize operations and profitability, and enhancing outcomes?
<--- Score

20. What is the recommended frequency of auditing?
<--- Score

21. How do senior leaders actions reflect a commitment to the organizations OT operational technology values?
<--- Score

22. Is knowledge gained on process shared and institutionalized?
<--- Score

23. Is there a OT operational technology Communication plan covering who needs to get what information when?
<--- Score

24. Is there documentation that will support the successful operation of the improvement?
<--- Score

25. Who sets the OT operational technology standards?
<--- Score

26. What can you control?
<--- Score

27. How do you establish and deploy modified action plans if circumstances require a shift in plans and rapid execution of new plans?
<--- Score

28. How can you best use all of your knowledge repositories to enhance learning and sharing?
<--- Score

29. What other areas of the group might benefit from

the OT operational technology team's improvements, knowledge, and learning?
<--- Score

30. What are your results for key measures or indicators of the accomplishment of your OT operational technology strategy and action plans, including building and strengthening core competencies?
<--- Score

31. Will the team be available to assist members in planning investigations?
<--- Score

32. You may have created your quality measures at a time when you lacked resources, technology wasn't up to the required standard, or low service levels were the industry norm. Have those circumstances changed?
<--- Score

33. Is a response plan in place for when the input, process, or output measures indicate an 'out-of-control' condition?
<--- Score

34. Will any special training be provided for results interpretation?
<--- Score

35. Is the OT operational technology test/monitoring cost justified?
<--- Score

36. How will the process owner verify improvement in

present and future sigma levels, process capabilities?
<--- Score

37. Is there a control plan in place for sustaining improvements (short and long-term)?
<--- Score

38. How will new or emerging customer needs/ requirements be checked/communicated to orient the process toward meeting the new specifications and continually reducing variation?
<--- Score

39. Is there a standardized process?
<--- Score

40. What do you measure to verify effectiveness gains?
<--- Score

41. How do your controls stack up?
<--- Score

42. Are the planned controls working?
<--- Score

43. Is a response plan established and deployed?
<--- Score

44. Are documented procedures clear and easy to follow for the operators?
<--- Score

45. How widespread is its use?
<--- Score

46. Are new process steps, standards, and documentation ingrained into normal operations?
<--- Score

47. Are operating procedures consistent?
<--- Score

48. Has the OT operational technology value of standards been quantified?
<--- Score

49. What quality tools were useful in the control phase?
<--- Score

50. In the case of a OT operational technology project, the criteria for the audit derive from implementation objectives, an audit of a OT operational technology project involves assessing whether the recommendations outlined for implementation have been met, can you track that any OT operational technology project is implemented as planned, and is it working?
<--- Score

51. Do the OT operational technology decisions you make today help people and the planet tomorrow?
<--- Score

52. What are the performance and scale of the OT operational technology tools?
<--- Score

53. How will input, process, and output variables be checked to detect for sub-optimal conditions?
<--- Score

54. What is the standard for acceptable OT operational technology performance?
<--- Score

55. Does the response plan contain a definite closed loop continual improvement scheme (e.g., plan-do-check-act)?
<--- Score

56. Is there a transfer of ownership and knowledge to process owner and process team tasked with the responsibilities.
<--- Score

57. Do you monitor the effectiveness of your OT operational technology activities?
<--- Score

58. Does job training on the documented procedures need to be part of the process team's education and training?
<--- Score

59. Who is the OT operational technology process owner?
<--- Score

60. Do you monitor the OT operational technology decisions made and fine tune them as they evolve?
<--- Score

61. What are customers monitoring?
<--- Score

62. How will OT operational technology decisions be

made and monitored?
<--- Score

63. What should the next improvement project be that is related to OT operational technology?
<--- Score

64. How do you plan on providing proper recognition and disclosure of supporting companies?
<--- Score

65. What are the critical parameters to watch?
<--- Score

66. How is change control managed?
<--- Score

67. Are the planned controls in place?
<--- Score

68. Will your goals reflect your program budget?
<--- Score

69. What is the control/monitoring plan?
<--- Score

70. How will you measure your QA plan's effectiveness?
<--- Score

71. What do you stand for--and what are you against?
<--- Score

72. Are controls in place and consistently applied?
<--- Score

73. Has the improved process and its steps been standardized?
<--- Score

74. What adjustments to the strategies are needed?
<--- Score

75. What is your plan to assess your security risks?
<--- Score

76. Act/Adjust: What Do you Need to Do Differently?
<--- Score

77. What is the best design framework for OT operational technology organization now that, in a post industrial-age if the top-down, command and control model is no longer relevant?
<--- Score

78. How likely is the current OT operational technology plan to come in on schedule or on budget?
<--- Score

79. Can you adapt and adjust to changing OT operational technology situations?
<--- Score

80. Does the OT operational technology performance meet the customer's requirements?
<--- Score

81. Who is going to spread your message?
<--- Score

82. Can support from partners be adjusted?

<--- Score

83. How will report readings be checked to effectively monitor performance?
<--- Score

84. What are the known security controls?
<--- Score

85. What do your reports reflect?
<--- Score

86. Is new knowledge gained imbedded in the response plan?
<--- Score

87. Are the OT operational technology standards challenging?
<--- Score

88. Does OT operational technology appropriately measure and monitor risk?
<--- Score

89. Who has control over resources?
<--- Score

90. Are suggested corrective/restorative actions indicated on the response plan for known causes to problems that might surface?
<--- Score

91. Does a troubleshooting guide exist or is it needed?
<--- Score

92. How do you select, collect, align, and integrate

OT operational technology data and information for tracking daily operations and overall organizational performance, including progress relative to strategic objectives and action plans?
<--- Score

93. Is reporting being used or needed?
<--- Score

94. Implementation Planning: is a pilot needed to test the changes before a full roll out occurs?
<--- Score

95. How will the process owner and team be able to hold the gains?
<--- Score

96. What is your theory of human motivation, and how does your compensation plan fit with that view?
<--- Score

97. Will existing staff require re-training, for example, to learn new business processes?
<--- Score

98. How do you plan for the cost of succession?
<--- Score

99. Against what alternative is success being measured?
<--- Score

100. Where do ideas that reach policy makers and planners as proposals for OT operational technology strengthening and reform actually originate?
<--- Score

101. Have new or revised work instructions resulted?
<--- Score

Add up total points for this section:
_____ = Total points for this section

Divided by: _____ (number of
statements answered) = _____
Average score for this section

Transfer your score to the OT
operational technology Index at the
beginning of the Self-Assessment.

CRITERION #7: SUSTAIN:

INTENT: Retain the benefits.

In my belief, the answer to this question is clearly defined:

5 Strongly Agree

4 Agree

3 Neutral

2 Disagree

1 Strongly Disagree

1. Do you have enough freaky customers in your portfolio pushing you to the limit day in and day out?
<--- Score

2. Why will customers want to buy your organizations products/services?
<--- Score

3. What assets are you most concerned about from a cybersecurity perspective?
<--- Score

4. What are strategies for increasing support and reducing opposition?
<--- Score

5. How do you manage OT operational technology Knowledge Management (KM)?
<--- Score

6. Instead of going to current contacts for new ideas, what if you reconnected with dormant contacts-- the people you used to know? If you were going reactivate a dormant tie, who would it be?
<--- Score

7. Would you rather sell to knowledgeable and informed customers or to uninformed customers?
<--- Score

8. Will there be any necessary staff changes (redundancies or new hires)?
<--- Score

9. Whom among your colleagues do you trust, and for what?
<--- Score

10. What is an unauthorized commitment?
<--- Score

11. What is the source of the strategies for OT operational technology strengthening and reform?
<--- Score

12. Do you have past OT operational technology successes?

<--- Score

13. What are you challenging?
<--- Score

14. Are the assumptions believable and achievable?
<--- Score

15. Are new benefits received and understood?
<--- Score

16. How do you listen to customers to obtain actionable information?
<--- Score

17. What OT operational technology skills are most important?
<--- Score

18. If you weren't already in this business, would you enter it today? And if not, what are you going to do about it?
<--- Score

19. Are all key stakeholders present at all Structured Walkthroughs?
<--- Score

20. Which functions and people interact with the supplier and or customer?
<--- Score

21. Why is it important to have senior management support for a OT operational technology project?
<--- Score

22. Is maximizing OT operational technology protection the same as minimizing OT operational technology loss?
<--- Score

23. Is your supply chain vulnerable?
<--- Score

24. How do you keep records, of what?
<--- Score

25. How do you foster the skills, knowledge, talents, attributes, and characteristics you want to have?
<--- Score

26. Where can you break convention?
<--- Score

27. Are assumptions made in OT operational technology stated explicitly?
<--- Score

28. What new services of functionality will be implemented next with OT operational technology ?
<--- Score

29. How do you go about securing OT operational technology?
<--- Score

30. Is there any reason to believe the opposite of my current belief?
<--- Score

31. Do you have the right people on the bus?
<--- Score

32. Which models, tools and techniques are necessary?
<--- Score

33. Is it economical; do you have the time and money?
<--- Score

34. Who do you think the world wants your organization to be?
<--- Score

35. Who will determine interim and final deadlines?
<--- Score

36. What would you recommend your friend do if he/she were facing this dilemma?
<--- Score

37. What are current OT operational technology paradigms?
<--- Score

38. What is effective OT operational technology?
<--- Score

39. Who else should you help?
<--- Score

40. How do you engage the workforce, in addition to satisfying them?
<--- Score

41. If there were zero limitations, what would you do differently?
<--- Score

42. How do you cross-sell and up-sell your OT operational technology success?
<--- Score

43. What information is critical to your organization that your executives are ignoring?
<--- Score

44. Do you think OT operational technology accomplishes the goals you expect it to accomplish?
<--- Score

45. Who is responsible for ensuring appropriate resources (time, people and money) are allocated to OT operational technology?
<--- Score

46. If you got fired and a new hire took your place, what would she do different?
<--- Score

47. What potential megatrends could make your business model obsolete?
<--- Score

48. What have you done to protect your business from competitive encroachment?
<--- Score

49. Will it be accepted by users?
<--- Score

50. How will you know that the OT operational technology project has been successful?
<--- Score

51. How does OT operational technology integrate with other stakeholder initiatives?
<--- Score

52. Who do we want your customers to become?
<--- Score

53. What is the overall talent health of your organization as a whole at senior levels, and for each organization reporting to a member of the Senior Leadership Team?
<--- Score

54. Can you do all this work?
<--- Score

55. Ask yourself: how would you do this work if you only had one staff member to do it?
<--- Score

56. Political -is anyone trying to undermine this project?
<--- Score

57. How do you govern and fulfill your societal responsibilities?
<--- Score

58. How can you negotiate OT operational technology successfully with a stubborn boss, an irate client, or a deceitful coworker?
<--- Score

59. Do you have the right capabilities and capacities?
<--- Score

60. Is a OT operational technology breakthrough on the horizon?

<--- Score

61. Is the impact that OT operational technology has shown?

<--- Score

62. Do you think you know, or do you know you know ?

<--- Score

63. Has implementation been effective in reaching specified objectives so far?

<--- Score

64. What counts that you are not counting?

<--- Score

65. How can you become the company that would put you out of business?

<--- Score

66. What business benefits will OT operational technology goals deliver if achieved?

<--- Score

67. At what moment would you think; Will I get fired?

<--- Score

68. How do you proactively clarify deliverables and OT operational technology quality expectations?

<--- Score

69. How do you keep the momentum going?

<--- Score

70. Can the schedule be done in the given time?
<--- Score

71. Who, on the executive team or the board, has spoken to a customer recently?
<--- Score

72. How do senior leaders deploy your organizations vision and values through your leadership system, to the workforce, to key suppliers and partners, and to customers and other stakeholders, as appropriate?
<--- Score

73. What happens if you do not have enough funding?
<--- Score

74. Do you say no to customers for no reason?
<--- Score

75. Why is OT operational technology important for you now?
<--- Score

76. What are the challenges?
<--- Score

77. How much contingency will be available in the budget?
<--- Score

78. How do customers see your organization?
<--- Score

79. What is your competitive advantage?
<--- Score

80. What will be the consequences to the stakeholder (financial, reputation etc) if OT operational technology does not go ahead or fails to deliver the objectives?
<--- Score

81. What is your question? Why?
<--- Score

82. How is implementation research currently incorporated into each of your goals?
<--- Score

83. Are you changing as fast as the world around you?
<--- Score

84. How do you track customer value, profitability or financial return, organizational success, and sustainability?
<--- Score

85. Is there a work around that you can use?
<--- Score

86. What are the long-term OT operational technology goals?
<--- Score

87. Can you break it down?
<--- Score

88. What are the barriers to increased OT operational technology production?
<--- Score

89. Who is on the team?
<--- Score

90. Is your basic point _____ or _____?
<--- Score

91. What are the key enablers to make this OT operational technology move?
<--- Score

92. Who are the key stakeholders?
<--- Score

93. What is your OT operational technology strategy?
<--- Score

94. Do you see more potential in people than they do in themselves?
<--- Score

95. If no one would ever find out about your accomplishments, how would you lead differently?
<--- Score

96. What are your most important goals for the strategic OT operational technology objectives?
<--- Score

97. What is a feasible sequencing of reform initiatives over time?
<--- Score

98. Is OT operational technology dependent on the successful delivery of a current project?
<--- Score

99. How can you become more high-tech but still be high touch?
<--- Score

100. How do you assess the OT operational technology pitfalls that are inherent in implementing it?
<--- Score

101. What is the kind of project structure that would be appropriate for your OT operational technology project, should it be formal and complex, or can it be less formal and relatively simple?
<--- Score

102. If your customer were your grandmother, would you tell her to buy what you're selling?
<--- Score

103. How do you create buy-in?
<--- Score

104. In the past year, what have you done (or could you have done) to increase the accurate perception of your company/brand as ethical and honest?
<--- Score

105. What unique value proposition (UVP) do you offer?
<--- Score

106. How do you know if you are successful?
<--- Score

107. How do you stay inspired?

<--- Score

108. What are specific OT operational technology rules to follow?
<--- Score

109. How do you provide a safe environment -physically and emotionally?
<--- Score

110. What have been your experiences in defining long range OT operational technology goals?
<--- Score

111. How do you make it meaningful in connecting OT operational technology with what users do day-to-day?
<--- Score

112. Is OT operational technology realistic, or are you setting yourself up for failure?
<--- Score

113. What are the essentials of internal OT operational technology management?
<--- Score

114. What are your personal philosophies regarding OT operational technology and how do they influence your work?
<--- Score

115. How do you ensure that implementations of OT operational technology products are done in a way that ensures safety?
<--- Score

116. Do OT operational technology rules make a reasonable demand on a users capabilities?
<--- Score

117. What are the success criteria that will indicate that OT operational technology objectives have been met and the benefits delivered?
<--- Score

118. Whose voice (department, ethnic group, women, older workers, etc) might you have missed hearing from in your company, and how might you amplify this voice to create positive momentum for your business?
<--- Score

119. Do you have an implicit bias for capital investments over people investments?
<--- Score

120. Is a OT operational technology team work effort in place?
<--- Score

121. Why should you adopt a OT operational technology framework?
<--- Score

122. Are you satisfied with your current role? If not, what is missing from it?
<--- Score

123. What may be the consequences for the performance of an organization if all stakeholders are not consulted regarding OT operational technology?

<--- Score

124. Do you know who is a friend or a foe?
<--- Score

125. How do you accomplish your long range OT operational technology goals?
<--- Score

126. What do we do when new problems arise?
<--- Score

127. Do you feel that more should be done in the OT operational technology area?
<--- Score

128. What is the overall business strategy?
<--- Score

129. Have new benefits been realized?
<--- Score

130. What is your BATNA (best alternative to a negotiated agreement)?
<--- Score

131. What is the big OT operational technology idea?
<--- Score

132. What threat is OT operational technology addressing?
<--- Score

133. How long will it take to change?
<--- Score

134. Who do you want your customers to become?
<--- Score

135. How do you lead with OT operational technology in mind?
<--- Score

136. How will you ensure you get what you expected?
<--- Score

137. In retrospect, of the projects that you pulled the plug on, what percent do you wish had been allowed to keep going, and what percent do you wish had ended earlier?
<--- Score

138. Have benefits been optimized with all key stakeholders?
<--- Score

139. How do you transition from the baseline to the target?
<--- Score

140. What knowledge, skills and characteristics mark a good OT operational technology project manager?
<--- Score

141. What trouble can you get into?
<--- Score

142. What was the last experiment you ran?
<--- Score

143. Are the criteria for selecting recommendations stated?

<--- Score

144. Which OT operational technology goals are the most important?
<--- Score

145. If you had to leave your organization for a year and the only communication you could have with employees/colleagues was a single paragraph, what would you write?
<--- Score

146. If you had to rebuild your organization without any traditional competitive advantages (i.e., no killer technology, promising research, innovative product/ service delivery model, etcetera), how would your people have to approach their work and collaborate together in order to create the necessary conditions for success?
<--- Score

147. Are you making progress, and are you making progress as OT operational technology leaders?
<--- Score

148. Why should people listen to you?
<--- Score

149. What is the craziest thing you can do?
<--- Score

150. Why not do OT operational technology?
<--- Score

151. What are the rules and assumptions your industry operates under? What if the opposite were true?

<--- Score

152. How will you insure seamless interoperability of OT operational technology moving forward?
<--- Score

153. What should you stop doing?
<--- Score

154. What one word do you want to own in the minds of your customers, employees, and partners?
<--- Score

155. Think of your OT operational technology project, what are the main functions?
<--- Score

156. What must you excel at?
<--- Score

157. What is the purpose of OT operational technology in relation to the mission?
<--- Score

158. How will you motivate the stakeholders with the least vested interest?
<--- Score

159. What are the top 3 things at the forefront of your OT operational technology agendas for the next 3 years?
<--- Score

160. What is the range of capabilities?
<--- Score

161. Do you know what you are doing? And who do you call if you don't?

<--- Score

162. Who is responsible for OT operational technology?

<--- Score

163. Who will manage the integration of tools?

<--- Score

164. What goals did you miss?

<--- Score

165. What are the business goals OT operational technology is aiming to achieve?

<--- Score

166. Can you maintain your growth without detracting from the factors that have contributed to your success?

<--- Score

167. When it comes to the industrial sector, why are so few asking about industrial cybersecurity?

<--- Score

168. Is there any existing OT operational technology governance structure?

<--- Score

169. What is something you believe that nearly no one agrees with you on?

<--- Score

170. Who have you, as a company, historically been

when you've been at your best?
<--- Score

171. What happens when a new employee joins the organization?
<--- Score

172. How do you determine the key elements that affect OT operational technology workforce satisfaction, how are these elements determined for different workforce groups and segments?
<--- Score

173. How are you doing compared to your industry?
<--- Score

174. Are you relevant? Will you be relevant five years from now? Ten?
<--- Score

175. Which individuals, teams or departments will be involved in OT operational technology?
<--- Score

176. How do you deal with OT operational technology changes?
<--- Score

177. Marketing budgets are tighter, consumers are more skeptical, and social media has changed forever the way we talk about OT operational technology, how do you gain traction?
<--- Score

178. How likely is it that a customer would recommend your company to a friend or colleague?

<--- Score

179. Who is responsible for errors?
<--- Score

180. How much does OT operational technology help?
<--- Score

181. Who uses your product in ways you never expected?
<--- Score

182. Who will provide the final approval of OT operational technology deliverables?
<--- Score

183. Were lessons learned captured and communicated?
<--- Score

184. What did you miss in the interview for the worst hire you ever made?
<--- Score

185. What is the funding source for this project?
<--- Score

186. To whom do you add value?
<--- Score

187. If your company went out of business tomorrow, would anyone who doesn't get a paycheck here care?
<--- Score

188. Are there any activities that you can take off your to do list?

<--- Score

189. What you are going to do to affect the numbers?
<--- Score

190. If you were responsible for initiating and implementing major changes in your organization, what steps might you take to ensure acceptance of those changes?
<--- Score

191. Did your employees make progress today?
<--- Score

192. What relationships among OT operational technology trends do you perceive?
<--- Score

193. Are your responses positive or negative?
<--- Score

194. What are the short and long-term OT operational technology goals?
<--- Score

195. Are you maintaining a past–present–future perspective throughout the OT operational technology discussion?
<--- Score

196. Is your organization prepared for the connected enterprise?
<--- Score

197. Are you paying enough attention to the partners your company depends on to succeed?

<--- Score

198. What does your signature ensure?
<--- Score

199. What trophy do you want on your mantle?
<--- Score

200. How do you maintain OT operational technology's Integrity?
<--- Score

201. What are you trying to prove to yourself, and how might it be hijacking your life and business success?
<--- Score

202. What is your formula for success in OT operational technology ?
<--- Score

203. What are the gaps in your knowledge and experience?
<--- Score

204. How important is OT operational technology to the user organizations mission?
<--- Score

205. What would have to be true for the option on the table to be the best possible choice?
<--- Score

206. How can you incorporate support to ensure safe and effective use of OT operational technology into the services that you provide?
<--- Score

207. How do you foster innovation?
<--- Score

208. What projects are going on in the organization today, and what resources are those projects using from the resource pools?
<--- Score

209. What is it like to work for you?
<--- Score

210. What stupid rule would you most like to kill?
<--- Score

211. Who will be responsible for deciding whether OT operational technology goes ahead or not after the initial investigations?
<--- Score

212. What are the potential basics of OT operational technology fraud?
<--- Score

213. What role does communication play in the success or failure of a OT operational technology project?
<--- Score

214. Why do and why don't your customers like your organization?
<--- Score

215. Is the OT operational technology organization completing tasks effectively and efficiently?
<--- Score

216. What are the usability implications of OT operational technology actions?
<--- Score

217. Are you / should you be revolutionary or evolutionary?
<--- Score

Add up total points for this section:
_____ = Total points for this section

Divided by: _____ (number of statements answered) = _____
Average score for this section

Transfer your score to the OT operational technology Index at the beginning of the Self-Assessment.

OT operational technology and Managing Projects, Criteria for Project Managers:

1.0 Initiating Process Group: OT operational technology

1. If the risk event occurs, what will you do?

2. What input will you be required to provide the OT operational technology project team?

3. What will be the pressing issues of tomorrow?

4. What do you need to do?

5. What areas were overlooked on this OT operational technology project?

6. Who is performing the work of the OT operational technology project?

7. Who does what?

8. What are the tools and techniques to be used in each phase?

9. Who is funding the OT operational technology project?

10. Are the changes in your OT operational technology project being formally requested, analyzed, and approved by the appropriate decision makers?

11. Does the OT operational technology project team have enough people to execute the OT operational technology project plan?

12. Mitigate. what will you do to minimize the impact should the risk event occur?

13. Were decisions made in a timely manner?

14. Are there resources to maintain and support the outcome of the OT operational technology project?

15. What are the overarching issues of your organization?

16. How well defined and documented were the OT operational technology project management processes you chose to use?

17. When will the OT operational technology project be done?

18. What communication items need improvement?

19. Establishment of pm office?

20. What will you do?

1.1 Project Charter: OT operational technology

21. Pop quiz – which are the same inputs as in the OT operational technology project charter?

22. Who is the sponsor?

23. What is the business need?

24. If finished, on what date did it finish?

25. When is a charter needed?

26. OT operational technology project objective statement: what must the OT operational technology project do?

27. Why Outsource?

28. Are you building in-house ?

29. What are the constraints?

30. What changes can you make to improve?

31. Where does all this information come from?

32. How high should you set your goals?

33. OT operational technology project background: what is the primary motivation for this OT operational technology project?

34. Are there special technology requirements?

35. Why have you chosen the aim you have set forth?

36. How much?

37. Is time of the essence?

38. Who ise input and support will this OT operational technology project require?

39. Assumptions and constraints: what assumptions were made in defining the OT operational technology project?

40. Name and describe the elements that deal with providing the detail?

1.2 Stakeholder Register: OT operational technology

41. Is your organization ready for change?

42. Who are the stakeholders?

43. What opportunities exist to provide communications?

44. How will reports be created?

45. Who wants to talk about Security?

46. How should employers make voices heard?

47. What is the power of the stakeholder?

48. How big is the gap?

49. Who is managing stakeholder engagement?

50. What are the major OT operational technology project milestones requiring communications or providing communications opportunities?

51. How much influence do they have on the OT operational technology project?

52. What & Why?

1.3 Stakeholder Analysis Matrix: OT operational technology

53. Processes, systems, it, communications?

54. Partnerships, agencies, distribution?

55. What is relationship with the OT operational technology project?

56. What is the range you need to look at?

57. Who is directly responsible for decisions on issues important to the OT operational technology project?

58. Do any safeguard policies apply to the OT operational technology project?

59. Who will be responsible for managing the outcome?

60. Geographical, export, import?

61. What coalitions might build around the issues being tackled?

62. Would it be fair to say that cost is a controlling criteria?

63. How can you counter negative efforts?

64. Does your organization have bad debt or cash-flow problems?

65. What do people from other organizations see as your strengths?

66. If the baseline is now, and if its improved it will be better than now?

67. How to involve media?

68. Economy - home, abroad?

69. Lack of competitive strength?

70. Are there people who ise voices or interests in the issue may not be heard?

71. How to measure the achievement of the Development Objective?

72. Who will be affected by the OT operational technology project?

2.0 Planning Process Group: OT operational technology

73. Did you read it correctly?

74. Is the duration of the program sufficient to ensure a cycle that will OT operational technology project the sustainability of the interventions?

75. Will the products created live up to the necessary quality?

76. Who are the OT operational technology project stakeholders?

77. If you are late, will anybody notice?

78. What business situation is being addressed?

79. Is the pace of implementing the products of the program ensuring the completeness of the results of the OT operational technology project?

80. Does it make any difference if you are successful?

81. Why is it important to determine activity sequencing on OT operational technology projects?

82. How well will the chosen processes produce the expected results?

83. To what extent have the target population and participants made the activities own, taking an active

role in it?

84. Mitigate. what will you do to minimize the impact should a risk event occur?

85. In what way has the program contributed towards the issue culture and development included on the public agenda?

86. What is a Software Development Life Cycle (SDLC)?

87. How does activity resource estimation affect activity duration estimation?

88. Product breakdown structure (pbs): what is the OT operational technology project result or product, and how should it look like, what are its parts?

89. Just how important is your work to the overall success of the OT operational technology project?

90. How are it OT operational technology projects different?

91. What are the different approaches to building the WBS?

2.1 Project Management Plan: OT operational technology

92. What did not work so well?

93. What is the justification?

94. Are there any client staffing expectations?

95. What goes into your OT operational technology project Charter?

96. What if, for example, the positive direction and vision of your organization causes expected trends to change resulting in greater need than expected?

97. Is the engineering content at a feasibility level-of-detail, and is it sufficiently complete, to provide an adequate basis for the baseline cost estimate?

98. What should you drop in order to add something new?

99. How do you manage time?

100. Who is the OT operational technology project Manager?

101. Is there an incremental analysis/cost effectiveness analysis of proposed mitigation features based on an approved method and using an accepted model?

102. What worked well?

103. How do you manage integration?

104. Are there non-structural buyout or relocation recommendations?

105. How can you best help your organization to develop consistent practices in OT operational technology project management planning stages?

106. What does management expect of PMs?

107. What would you do differently what did not work?

108. Has the selected plan been formulated using cost effectiveness and incremental analysis techniques?

109. What happened during the process that you found interesting?

110. What is OT operational technology project scope management?

111. What are the assigned resources?

2.2 Scope Management Plan: OT operational technology

112. Has process improvement efforts been completed before requirements efforts begin?

113. Are milestone deliverables effectively tracked and compared to OT operational technology project plan?

114. Is there any form of automated support for Issues Management?

115. Where do scope processes fit in?

116. Will your organizations estimating methodology be used and followed?

117. Have adequate procedures been put in place for OT operational technology project communication and status reporting across OT operational technology project boundaries (for example interdependent software development among interfacing systems)?

118. What does the critical path really mean?

119. What do you need to do to accomplish the goal or goals?

120. Is there an on-going process in place to monitor OT operational technology project risks?

121. Are the payment terms being followed?

122. Are meeting minutes captured and sent out after the meeting?

123. Do you have funding for OT operational technology project and product development, implementation and on-going support?

124. What are the risks that could significantly affect the budget of the OT operational technology project?

125. Organizational policies that might affect the availability of resources?

126. Are software metrics formally captured, analyzed and used as a basis for other OT operational technology project estimates?

127. Are OT operational technology project contact logs kept up to date?

128. Are you meeting with stake holders and team members?

129. Are issues raised, assessed, actioned, and resolved in a timely and efficient manner?

130. Would the OT operational technology project cost sharing involve reimbursement to the sponsor?

131. Have the key functions and capabilities been defined and assigned to each release or iteration?

2.3 Requirements Management Plan: OT operational technology

132. Do you have an agreed upon process for alerting the OT operational technology project Manager if a request for change in requirements leads to a product scope change?

133. Will the OT operational technology project requirements become approved in writing?

134. Why manage requirements?

135. Who will do the reporting and to whom will reports be delivered?

136. Is the system software (non-operating system) new to the IT OT operational technology project team?

137. What went right?

138. Did you get proper approvals?

139. Do you understand the role that each stakeholder will play in the requirements process?

140. Who has the authority to reject OT operational technology project requirements?

141. What cost metrics will be used?

142. Is the change control process documented?

143. Is requirements work dependent on any other specific OT operational technology project or non-OT operational technology project activities (e.g. funding, approvals, procurement)?

144. Will the contractors involved take full responsibility?

145. If it exists, where is it housed?

146. Is it new or replacing an existing business system or process?

147. Will you use tracing to help understand the impact of a change in requirements?

148. What is the earliest finish date for this OT operational technology project if it is scheduled to start on ...?

149. Will you have access to stakeholders when you need them?

150. To see if a requirement statement is sufficiently well-defined, read it from the developers perspective. Mentally add the phrase, call me when youre done to the end of the requirement and see if that makes you nervous. In other words, would you need additional clarification from the author to understand the requirement well enough to design and implement it?

151. The wbs is developed as part of a joint planning session. and how do you know that youhave done this right?

2.4 Requirements Documentation: OT operational technology

152. How does the proposed OT operational technology project contribute to the overall objectives of your organization?

153. How much does requirements engineering cost?

154. What facilities must be supported by the system?

155. How will requirements be documented and who signs off on them?

156. How do you know when a Requirement is accurate enough?

157. Consistency. are there any requirements conflicts?

158. Are there any requirements conflicts?

159. Who is involved?

160. How linear / iterative is your Requirements Gathering process (or will it be)?

161. What is a show stopper in the requirements?

162. What variations exist for a process?

163. What can tools do for us?

164. Can you check system requirements?

165. What are the acceptance criteria?

166. Who is interacting with the system?

167. Have the benefits identified with the system being identified clearly?

168. Completeness. are all functions required by the customer included?

169. What is the risk associated with cost and schedule?

170. Are there legal issues?

171. Can the requirement be changed without a large impact on other requirements?

2.5 Requirements Traceability Matrix: OT operational technology

172. Why use a WBS?

173. What percentage of OT operational technology projects are producing traceability matrices between requirements and other work products?

174. Will you use a Requirements Traceability Matrix?

175. What is the WBS?

176. How will it affect the stakeholders personally in career?

177. Why do you manage scope?

178. Is there a requirements traceability process in place?

179. Describe the process for approving requirements so they can be added to the traceability matrix and OT operational technology project work can be performed. Will the OT operational technology project requirements become approved in writing?

180. How small is small enough?

181. How do you manage scope?

182. Do you have a clear understanding of all subcontracts in place?

183. What are the chronologies, contingencies, consequences, criteria?

2.6 Project Scope Statement: OT operational technology

184. Any new risks introduced or old risks impacted. Are there issues that could affect the existing requirements for the result, service, or product if the scope changes?

185. Will the risk plan be updated on a regular and frequent basis?

186. Are there adequate OT operational technology project control systems?

187. What is change?

188. Is there a Quality Assurance Plan documented and filed?

189. Will the qa related information be reported regularly as part of the status reporting mechanisms?

190. Are the meetings set up to have assigned note takers that will add action/issues to the issue list?

191. Is there a process (test plans, inspections, reviews) defined for verifying outputs for each task?

192. OT operational technology project lead, team lead, solution architect?

193. Is the plan for OT operational technology project resources adequate?

194. Were key OT operational technology project stakeholders brought into the OT operational technology project Plan?

195. Will tasks be marked complete only after QA has been successfully completed?

196. Will there be a Change Control Process in place?

197. How will you verify the accuracy of the work of the OT operational technology project, and what constitutes acceptance of the deliverables?

198. Elements that deal with providing the detail?

199. Elements of scope management that deal with concept development ?

200. Identify how your team and you will create the OT operational technology project scope statement and the work breakdown structure (WBS). Document how you will create the OT operational technology project scope statement and WBS, and make sure you answer the following questions: In defining OT operational technology project scope and the WBS, will you and your OT operational technology project team be using methods defined by your organization, methods defined by the OT operational technology project management office (PMO), or other methods?

201. Is the OT operational technology project organization documented and on file?

2.7 Assumption and Constraint Log: OT operational technology

202. Have all necessary approvals been obtained?

203. What strengths do you have?

204. Security analysis has access to information that is sanitized?

205. What weaknesses do you have?

206. Is there documentation of system capability requirements, data requirements, environment requirements, security requirements, and computer and hardware requirements?

207. Are there standards for code development?

208. Are there cosmetic errors that hinder readability and comprehension?

209. Contradictory information between different documents?

210. Do documented requirements exist for all critical components and areas, including technical, business, interfaces, performance, security and conversion requirements?

211. Diagrams and tables are included to account for complex concepts and increase overall readability?

212. After observing execution of process, is it in compliance with the documented Plan?

213. Are formal code reviews conducted?

214. How do you design an auditing system?

215. How can constraints be violated?

216. Are there processes in place to ensure that all the terms and code concepts have been documented consistently?

217. How many OT operational technology project staff does this specific process affect?

218. What does an audit system look like?

219. Have all stakeholders been identified?

220. Do you know what your customers expectations are regarding this process?

2.8 Work Breakdown Structure: OT operational technology

221. When do you stop?

222. How many levels?

223. Where does it take place?

224. What is the probability that the OT operational technology project duration will exceed xx weeks?

225. When does it have to be done?

226. Is it still viable?

227. How will you and your OT operational technology project team define the OT operational technology projects scope and work breakdown structure?

228. Why would you develop a Work Breakdown Structure?

229. What is the probability of completing the OT operational technology project in less that xx days?

230. Why is it useful?

231. How far down?

232. How big is a work-package?

233. Is the work breakdown structure (wbs) defined and is the scope of the OT operational technology project clear with assigned deliverable owners?

234. What has to be done?

235. Who has to do it?

236. Is it a change in scope?

237. Can you make it?

2.9 WBS Dictionary: OT operational technology

238. Are the overhead pools formally and adequately identified?

239. Are detailed work packages planned as far in advance as practicable?

240. Are estimates of costs at completion utilized in determining contract funding requirements and reporting them?

241. Are records maintained to show how management reserves are used?

242. Does the accounting system provide a basis for auditing records of direct costs chargeable to the contract?

243. Does the contractors system description or procedures require that the performance measurement baseline plus management reserve equal the contract budget base?

244. Changes in the direct base to which overhead costs are allocated?

245. Are records maintained to show how undistributed budgets are controlled?

246. Evaluate the performance of operating organizations?

247. Does the contractors system identify work accomplishment against the schedule plan?

248. Are data elements summarized through the functional organizational structure for progressively higher levels of management?

249. Major functional areas of contract effort?

250. Performance to date and material commitment?

251. Are indirect costs charged to the appropriate indirect pools and incurring organization?

252. Changes in the nature of the overhead requirements?

253. Wbs elements contractually specified for reporting of status to you (lowest level only)?

254. Is the entire contract planned in time-phased control accounts to the extent practicable?

255. Contractor financial periods; for example, annual?

256. Budgeted cost for work performed?

2.10 Schedule Management Plan: OT operational technology

257. Is a pmo (OT operational technology project management office) in place and provide oversight to the OT operational technology project?

258. Perform reality checks on schedules – are all tasks included?

259. What does a valid Schedule look like?

260. Pareto diagrams, statistical sampling, flow charting or trend analysis used quality monitoring?

261. Has a resource management plan been created?

262. What will be the format of the schedule model?

263. Is there anything planned that does not need to be here?

264. Do OT operational technology project managers participating in the OT operational technology project know the OT operational technology projects true status first hand?

265. Does the business case include how the OT operational technology project aligns with your organizations strategic goals & objectives?

266. Does the ims reflect accurate current status and credible start/finish forecasts for all to-go tasks and

milestones?

267. Is there an onboarding process in place?

268. Are the people assigned to the OT operational technology project sufficiently qualified?

269. Are changes in scope (deliverable commitments) agreed to by all affected groups & individuals?

270. Are all activities logically sequenced?

271. Is there a procedure for management, control and release of schedule margin?

272. Are OT operational technology project contact logs kept up to date?

273. Is the quality assurance team identified?

274. Is the ims used by all levels of management for OT operational technology project implementation and control?

275. Where is the scheduling tool and who has access to it to view it?

2.11 Activity List: OT operational technology

276. Is infrastructure setup part of your OT operational technology project?

277. How detailed should a OT operational technology project get?

278. Should you include sub-activities?

279. Can you determine the activity that must finish, before this activity can start?

280. What did not go as well?

281. What is the probability the OT operational technology project can be completed in xx weeks?

282. What are you counting on?

283. Who will perform the work?

284. What went well?

285. For other activities, how much delay can be tolerated?

286. What will be performed?

287. Are the required resources available or need to be acquired?

288. What is your organizations history in doing similar activities?

289. When will the work be performed?

290. What went wrong?

291. How will it be performed?

292. In what sequence?

293. How difficult will it be to do specific activities on this OT operational technology project?

294. When do the individual activities need to start and finish?

2.12 Activity Attributes: OT operational technology

295. Can you re-assign any activities to another resource to resolve an over-allocation?

296. How much activity detail is required?

297. How difficult will it be to complete specific activities on this OT operational technology project?

298. Were there other ways you could have organized the data to achieve similar results?

299. What is the general pattern here?

300. Have constraints been applied to the start and finish milestones for the phases?

301. Are the required resources available?

302. How many days do you need to complete the work scope with a limit of X number of resources?

303. Activity: what is In the Bag?

304. Can more resources be added?

305. Have you identified the Activity Leveling Priority code value on each activity?

306. What is missing?

307. What conclusions/generalizations can you draw from this?

308. How else could the items be grouped?

309. Why?

310. Has management defined a definite timeframe for the turnaround or OT operational technology project window?

311. How difficult will it be to do specific activities on this OT operational technology project?

312. Do you feel very comfortable with your prediction?

2.13 Milestone List: OT operational technology

313. Describe the concept of the technology, product or service that will be or has been developed. How will it be used?

314. How soon can the activity start?

315. How will the milestone be verified?

316. New USPs?

317. Loss of key staff?

318. Level of the Innovation?

319. Which path is the critical path?

320. Reliability of data, plan predictability?

321. Sustainable financial backing?

322. Who will manage the OT operational technology project on a day-to-day basis?

323. It is to be a narrative text providing the crucial aspects of your OT operational technology project proposal answering what, who, how, when and where?

324. How late can each activity be finished and started?

325. Global influences?

326. Political effects?

327. What date will the task finish?

328. Competitive advantages?

329. Identify critical paths (one or more) and which activities are on the critical path?

330. What background experience, skills, and strengths does the team bring to your organization?

331. Do you foresee any technical risks or developmental challenges?

332. How late can the activity start?

2.14 Network Diagram: OT operational technology

333. What job or jobs could run concurrently?

334. Review the logical flow of the network diagram. Take a look at which activities you have first and then sequence the activities. Do they make sense?

335. What can be done concurrently?

336. What are the tools?

337. Can you calculate the confidence level?

338. Planning: who, how long, what to do?

339. Are the gantt chart and/or network diagram updated periodically and used to assess the overall OT operational technology project timetable?

340. Where do schedules come from?

341. What activity must be completed immediately before this activity can start?

342. What is the lowest cost to complete this OT operational technology project in xx weeks?

343. What job or jobs follow it?

344. Why must you schedule milestones, such as reviews, throughout the OT operational technology

project?

345. If the OT operational technology project network diagram cannot change and you have extra personnel resources, what is the BEST thing to do?

346. Where do you schedule uncertainty time?

347. What activities must occur simultaneously with this activity?

348. What to do and When?

349. If a current contract exists, can you provide the vendor name, contract start, and contract expiration date?

350. What activities must follow this activity?

351. What controls the start and finish of a job?

2.15 Activity Resource Requirements: OT operational technology

352. Organizational Applicability?

353. When does monitoring begin?

354. Do you use tools like decomposition and rolling-wave planning to produce the activity list and other outputs?

355. Are there unresolved issues that need to be addressed?

356. How do you handle petty cash?

357. Time for overtime?

358. Other support in specific areas?

359. How many signatures do you require on a check and does this match what is in your policy and procedures?

360. Which logical relationship does the PDM use most often?

361. Why do you do that?

362. Anything else?

363. What are constraints that you might find during the Human Resource Planning process?

364. What is the Work Plan Standard?

2.16 Resource Breakdown Structure: OT operational technology

365. What is the purpose of assigning and documenting responsibility?

366. How should the information be delivered?

367. What are the requirements for resource data?

368. Changes based on input from stakeholders?

369. Why do you do it?

370. Why time management?

371. Goals for the OT operational technology project. What is each stakeholders desired outcome for the OT operational technology project?

372. What is each stakeholders desired outcome for the OT operational technology project?

373. Who is allowed to see what data about which resources?

374. What is OT operational technology project communication management?

375. When do they need the information?

376. Who is allowed to perform which functions?

377. Who delivers the information?

378. What can you do to improve productivity?

379. The list could probably go on, but, the thing that you would most like to know is, How long & How much?

380. What defines a successful OT operational technology project?

2.17 Activity Duration Estimates: OT operational technology

381. What are key inputs and outputs of the software?

382. What are the main types of goods and services being outsourced?

383. Are contractor costs, schedule and technical performance monitored throughout the OT operational technology project?

384. What is the BEST thing for the OT operational technology project manager to do?

385. What is earned value?

386. How have experts such as Deming, Juran, Crosby, and Taguchi affected the quality movement and todays use of Six Sigma?

387. How could you define throughput and how would your organization benefit from maximizing it?

388. What are crucial elements of successful OT operational technology project plan execution?

389. What type of contract was used and why?

390. What does it mean to take a systems view of a OT operational technology project?

391. Are costs that may be needed to account for OT

operational technology project risks determined?

392. Consider the examples of poor quality in information technology OT operational technology projects presented in the What Went Wrong?

393. What are the advantages and disadvantages of PERT?

394. Do you agree with the suggestions provided for improving OT operational technology project communications?

395. Are measurement techniques employed to determine the potential impact of proposed changes?

396. What distinguishes one organization from another in this area?

397. When a risk event occurs, is the risk response evaluated and the appropriate response implemented?

398. What type of information goes in a quality assurance plan?

399. How difficult will it be to complete specific activities on this OT operational technology project?

400. Calculate the expected duration for an activity that has a most likely time of 3, a pessimistic time of 10, and a optimiztic time of 2?

2.18 Duration Estimating Worksheet: OT operational technology

401. Define the work as completely as possible. What work will be included in the OT operational technology project?

402. Is the OT operational technology project responsive to community need?

403. Why estimate costs?

404. What is the total time required to complete the OT operational technology project if no delays occur?

405. Small or large OT operational technology project?

406. What is an Average OT operational technology project?

407. Does the OT operational technology project provide innovative ways for stakeholders to overcome obstacles or deliver better outcomes?

408. Science = process: remember the scientific method?

409. Do any colleagues have experience with your organization and/or RFPs?

410. When, then?

411. How can the OT operational technology project be displayed graphically to better visualize the activities?

412. Is a construction detail attached (to aid in explanation)?

413. What utility impacts are there?

414. What are the critical bottleneck activities?

415. When does your organization expect to be able to complete it?

416. Is this operation cost effective?

417. Done before proceeding with this activity or what can be done concurrently?

418. What info is needed?

2.19 Project Schedule: OT operational technology

419. Are you working on the right risks?

420. How can you shorten the schedule?

421. Your OT operational technology project management plan results in a OT operational technology project schedule that is too long. If the OT operational technology project network diagram cannot change and you have extra personnel resources, what is the BEST thing to do?

422. Schedule/cost recovery?

423. Are the original OT operational technology project schedule and budget realistic?

424. What does that mean?

425. Why or why not?

426. It allows the OT operational technology project to be delivered on schedule. How Do you Use Schedules?

427. Why is this particularly bad?

428. Change management required?

429. How much slack is available in the OT operational technology project?

430. Should you have a test for each code module?

431. Is OT operational technology project work proceeding in accordance with the original OT operational technology project schedule?

432. Understand the constraints used in preparing the schedule. Are activities connected because logic dictates the order in which others occur?

433. How do you manage OT operational technology project Risk?

434. To what degree is do you feel the entire team was committed to the OT operational technology project schedule?

435. Are activities connected because logic dictates the order in which others occur?

436. Are key risk mitigation strategies added to the OT operational technology project schedule?

2.20 Cost Management Plan: OT operational technology

437. Is an industry recognized mechanized support tool(s) being used for OT operational technology project scheduling & tracking?

438. Designated small business reserve?

439. Are trade-offs between accepting the risk and mitigating the risk identified?

440. Have reserves been created to address risks?

441. What does this mean to a cost or scheduler manager?

442. Are updated OT operational technology project time & resource estimates reasonable based on the current OT operational technology project stage?

443. Have all involved OT operational technology project stakeholders and work groups committed to the OT operational technology project?

444. Are metrics used to evaluate and manage Vendors?

445. Mitigation – based on the action, cost and probability of success, will the mitigation be made?

446. Are estimating assumptions and constraints captured?

447. Is there a formal set of procedures supporting Stakeholder Management?

448. Are the schedule estimates reasonable given the OT operational technology project?

449. Quality assurance overheads?

450. Does the OT operational technology project have a formal OT operational technology project Charter?

451. Has the scope management document been updated and distributed to help prevent scope creep?

452. Is there an issues management plan in place?

453. Do OT operational technology project teams & team members report on status / activities / progress?

454. Staffing Requirements?

2.21 Activity Cost Estimates: OT operational technology

455. Estimated cost?

456. Does the estimator estimate by task or by person?

457. Where can you get activity reports?

458. What is the activity recast of the budget?

459. How do you change activities?

460. Can you delete activities or make them inactive?

461. What makes a good expected result statement?

462. Who & what determines the need for contracted services?

463. Measurable - are the targets measurable?

464. Would you hire them again?

465. Were escalated issues resolved promptly?

466. Who determines when the contractor is paid?

467. Which contract type places the most risk on the seller?

468. What areas does the group agree are the biggest

success on the OT operational technology project?

469. What is the activity inventory?

470. What cost data should be used to estimate costs during the 2-year follow-up period?

471. Are data needed on characteristics of care?

472. How many activities should you have?

473. What areas were overlooked on this OT operational technology project?

2.22 Cost Estimating Worksheet: OT operational technology

474. What is the estimated labor cost today based upon this information?

475. What will others want?

476. Does the OT operational technology project provide innovative ways for stakeholders to overcome obstacles or deliver better outcomes?

477. What is the purpose of estimating?

478. What can be included?

479. Is it feasible to establish a control group arrangement?

480. Who is best positioned to know and assist in identifying corresponding factors?

481. Is the OT operational technology project responsive to community need?

482. Value pocket identification & quantification what are value pockets?

483. What costs are to be estimated?

484. What additional OT operational technology project(s) could be initiated as a result of this OT operational technology project?

485. How will the results be shared and to whom?

486. Will the OT operational technology project collaborate with the local community and leverage resources?

487. Identify the timeframe necessary to monitor progress and collect data to determine how the selected measure has changed?

488. What happens to any remaining funds not used?

489. Ask: are others positioned to know, are others credible, and will others cooperate?

490. Can a trend be established from historical performance data on the selected measure and are the criteria for using trend analysis or forecasting methods met?

2.23 Cost Baseline: OT operational technology

491. What does a good WBS NOT look like?

492. Has the actual cost of the OT operational technology project (or OT operational technology project phase) been tallied and compared to the approved budget?

493. Should a more thorough impact analysis be conducted?

494. Where do changes come from?

495. How concrete were original objectives?

496. Will the OT operational technology project fail if the change request is not executed?

497. How will cost estimates be used?

498. On budget?

499. Have all approved changes to the cost baseline been identified and impact on the OT operational technology project documented?

500. Is the requested change request a result of changes in other OT operational technology project(s)?

501. Escalation criteria met?

502. At which frequency ?

503. Have the resources used by the OT operational technology project been reassigned to other units or OT operational technology projects?

504. What is the reality?

505. What deliverables come first?

506. Are procedures defined by which the cost baseline may be changed?

2.24 Quality Management Plan: OT operational technology

507. You know what your customers expectations are regarding this process?

508. Do trained quality assurance auditors conduct the audits as defined in the Quality Management Plan and scheduled by the OT operational technology project manager?

509. How do senior leaders review organizational performance?

510. Are there nonconformance issues?

511. How do senior leaders create your organizational focus on customers and other stakeholders?

512. Do the data quality objectives communicate the intended program need?

513. How are records kept in the office?

514. How are new requirements or changes to requirements identified?

515. Does the program use other agents to collect samples?

516. What is the Quality Management Plan?

517. Have OT operational technology project

management standards and procedures been established and documented?

518. How are senior leaders, employees, and your organization involved in supporting the community?

519. How does your organization manage work to promote cooperation, individual initiative, innovation, flexibility, communications, and knowledge/skill sharing across work units?

520. Can you perform this task or activity in a more effective manner?

521. Meet how often?

522. If it is out of compliance, should the process be amended or should the Plan be amended?

523. What procedures are used to determine if you use, and the number of split, replicate or duplicate samples taken at a site?

524. No superfluous information or marketing narrative?

525. Is staff trained on the software technologies that are being used on the OT operational technology project?

2.25 Quality Metrics: OT operational technology

526. What is the CMS Benchmark?

527. Did evaluation start on time?

528. Is there a set of procedures to capture, analyze and act on quality metrics?

529. What are your organizations expectations for its quality OT operational technology project?

530. Has it met internal or external standards?

531. When is the security analysis testing complete?

532. Was review conducted per standard protocols?

533. What are your organizations next steps?

534. How do you calculate corresponding metrics?

535. What happens if you get an abnormal result?

536. What group is empowered to define quality requirements?

537. Which data do others need in one place to target areas of improvement?

538. Did the team meet the OT operational technology project success criteria documented in

the Quality Metrics Matrix?

539. What method of measurement do you use?

540. Are quality metrics defined?

541. Where did complaints, returns and warranty claims come from?

542. What level of statistical confidence do you use?

543. Where is quality now?

2.26 Process Improvement Plan: OT operational technology

544. What actions are needed to address the problems and achieve the goals?

545. What personnel are the sponsors for that initiative?

546. Everyone agrees on what process improvement is, right?

547. Are you making progress on the improvement framework?

548. Have the frequency of collection and the points in the process where measurements will be made been determined?

549. Purpose of goal: the motive is determined by asking, why do you want to achieve this goal?

550. What is the test-cycle concept?

551. Are there forms and procedures to collect and record the data?

552. What lessons have you learned so far?

553. Why quality management?

554. What is the return on investment?

555. How do you measure?

556. Does your process ensure quality?

557. Modeling current processes is great, and will you ever see a return on that investment?

558. Where are you now?

559. Are you following the quality standards?

560. If a process improvement framework is being used, which elements will help the problems and goals listed?

561. The motive is determined by asking, Why do you want to achieve this goal?

562. What personnel are the champions for the initiative?

563. Where do you want to be?

2.27 Responsibility Assignment Matrix: OT operational technology

564. Most people let you know when others re too busy, and are others really too busy?

565. What are the deliverables?

566. Are authorized changes being incorporated in a timely manner?

567. Are there any drawbacks to using a responsibility assignment matrix?

568. What do you need to implement earned value management?

569. Are work packages assigned to performing organizations?

570. Budgeted cost for work scheduled?

571. Do you know how your people are allocated?

572. Are all authorized tasks assigned to identified organizational elements?

573. Is budgeted cost for work performed calculated in a manner consistent with the way work is planned?

574. Competencies and craftsmanship – what competencies are necessary and what level?

575. Changes in the current direct and OT operational technology projected base?

576. What expertise is not available in your department?

577. What expertise is available in your department?

578. What travel needed?

579. Will too many Communicating responsibilities tangle the OT operational technology project in unnecessary communications?

580. How can this help you with team building?

581. No rs: if a task has no one listed as responsible, who is getting the job done?

2.28 Roles and Responsibilities: OT operational technology

582. Required skills, knowledge, experience?

583. Influence: what areas of organizational decision making are you able to influence when you do not have authority to make the final decision?

584. What areas would you highlight for changes or improvements?

585. Who is responsible for implementation activities and where will the functions, roles and responsibilities be defined?

586. Where are you most strong as a supervisor?

587. To decide whether to use a quality measurement, ask how will you know when it is achieved?

588. What are your major roles and responsibilities in the area of performance measurement and assessment?

589. Authority: what areas/OT operational technology projects in your work do you have the authority to decide upon and act on the already stated decisions?

590. Are OT operational technology project team roles and responsibilities identified and documented?

591. What specific behaviors did you observe?

592. Does your vision/mission support a culture of quality data?

593. Is there a training program in place for stakeholders covering expectations, roles and responsibilities and any addition knowledge others need to be good stakeholders?

594. Is the data complete?

595. Was the expectation clearly communicated?

596. What should you do now to prepare for your career 5+ years from now?

597. What expectations were NOT met?

598. Concern: where are you limited or have no authority, where you can not influence?

599. Have you ever been a part of this team?

600. Are OT operational technology project team roles and responsibilities identified and documented?

2.29 Human Resource Management Plan: OT operational technology

601. Are all resource assumptions documented?

602. Is there a Quality Management Plan?

603. Do all stakeholders know how to access this repository and where to find the OT operational technology project documentation?

604. Have key stakeholders been identified?

605. What areas were overlooked on this OT operational technology project?

606. Are written status reports provided on a designated frequent basis?

607. Is a stakeholder management plan in place that covers topics?

608. Were OT operational technology project team members involved in the development of activity & task decomposition?

609. Are risk triggers captured?

610. What were things that you did very well and want to do the same again on the next OT operational technology project?

611. Does the schedule include OT operational

technology project management time and change request analysis time?

612. Has the budget been baselined?

613. Are the people assigned to the OT operational technology project sufficiently qualified?

614. Were OT operational technology project team members involved in detailed estimating and scheduling?

615. Are decisions captured in a decisions log?

616. Have process improvement efforts been completed before requirements efforts begin?

617. Has a quality assurance plan been developed for the OT operational technology project?

2.30 Communications Management Plan: OT operational technology

618. How did the term stakeholder originate?

619. Do you prepare stakeholder engagement plans?

620. Do you feel more overwhelmed by stakeholders?

621. What communications method?

622. What is the stakeholders level of authority?

623. Is there an important stakeholder who is actively opposed and will not receive messages?

624. Which stakeholders can influence others?

625. What is OT operational technology project communications management?

626. What approaches to you feel are the best ones to use?

627. Are there too many who have an interest in some aspect of your work?

628. What steps can you take for a positive relationship?

629. What help do you and your team need from the stakeholder?

630. Are there potential barriers between the team and the stakeholder?

631. Who are the members of the governing body?

632. Are the stakeholders getting the information others need, are others consulted, are concerns addressed?

633. Are stakeholders internal or external?

634. Who to learn from?

635. Are others needed?

636. What to learn?

637. Why manage stakeholders?

2.31 Risk Management Plan: OT operational technology

638. Have you worked with the customer in the past?

639. Where do risks appear in the business phases?

640. Was an original risk assessment/risk management plan completed?

641. What can you do to minimize the impact if it does?

642. What is the impact to the OT operational technology project if the item is not resolved in a timely fashion?

643. How are risk analvsis and prioritization performed?

644. Have customers been involved fully in the definition of requirements?

645. Is the customer willing to commit significant time to the requirements gathering process?

646. Are requirements fully understood by the software engineering team and customers?

647. Do requirements put excessive performance constraints on the product?

648. What things are likely to change?

649. Is the customer willing to establish rapid communication links with the developer?

650. What are the chances the event will occur?

651. What can go wrong?

652. Could others have been better mitigated?

653. Have staff received necessary training?

654. Are the metrics meaningful and useful?

655. What are some questions that should be addressed in a risk management plan?

656. Are certain activities taking a long time to complete?

657. How much risk can you tolerate?

2.32 Risk Register: OT operational technology

658. Assume the risk event or situation happens, what would the impact be?

659. What should you do now?

660. Preventative actions - planned actions to reduce the likelihood a risk will occur and/or reduce the seriousness should it occur. What should you do now?

661. What should you do when?

662. Assume the event happens, what is the Most Likely impact?

663. Risk documentation: what reporting formats and processes will be used for risk management activities?

664. Who needs to know about this?

665. Amongst the action plans and recommendations that you have to introduce are there some that could stop or delay the overall program?

666. When will it happen?

667. Market risk -will the new service or product be useful to your organization or marketable to others?

668. Financial risk -can your organization afford to undertake the OT operational technology project?

669. What are you going to do to limit the OT operational technology projects risk exposure due to the identified risks?

670. Are there other alternative controls that could be implemented?

671. What will be done?

672. What is a Risk?

673. What would the impact to the OT operational technology project objectives be should the risk arise?

674. Do you require further engagement?

675. What can be done about it?

676. Have other controls and solutions been implemented in other services which could be applied as an alternative to additional funding?

677. What are the assumptions and current status that support the assessment of the risk?

2.33 Probability and Impact Assessment: OT operational technology

678. Are tools for analysis and design available?

679. How would you suggest monitoring for risk transition indicators?

680. Are the software tools integrated with each other?

681. What will be the environmental impact of the OT operational technology project?

682. What are the levels of understanding of the future users of the outcome/results of this OT operational technology project?

683. Do you have specific methods that you use for each phase of the process?

684. What should be the requirement of organizational restructuring as each subOT operational technology project goes through a different lifecycle phase?

685. Can the OT operational technology project proceed without assuming the risk?

686. What is the likely future demand of the customer?

687. What are the preparations required for facing difficulties?

688. How is the risk management process used in practice?

689. Can this technology be absorbed with current level of expertise available in your organization?

690. How do you maximize short-term return on investment?

691. What are the current requirements of the customer?

692. What should be the level of coordination?

693. How risk averse are you?

694. Have top software and customer managers formally committed to support the OT operational technology project?

695. Does the software engineering team have the right mix of skills?

696. Has the need for the OT operational technology project been properly established?

697. Mitigation -how can you avoid the risk?

2.34 Probability and Impact Matrix: OT operational technology

698. Number of users of the product?

699. Who should be notified of the occurrence of each of the risk indicators?

700. What are the likely future requirements?

701. Management -what contingency plans do you have if the risk becomes a reality?

702. Can you handle the investment risk?

703. Is the OT operational technology project cutting across the entire organization?

704. What will be the likely political situation during the life of the OT operational technology project?

705. Which risks need to move on to Perform Quantitative Risk Analysis?

706. Costs associated with late delivery or a defective product?

707. What will be cost of redeployment of the personnel?

708. How are the local factors going to affect the absorption?

709. Do requirements demand the use of new analysis, design, or testing methods?

710. What are the levels of understanding of the future users of this technology?

711. What is the industrial relations prevailing in this organization?

712. To what extent is the chosen technology maturing?

713. What can you use the analyzed risks for?

714. If you can not fix it, how do you do it differently?

715. What should be the gestation period for the OT operational technology project with this technology?

2.35 Risk Data Sheet: OT operational technology

716. What is the likelihood of it happening?

717. If it happens, what are the consequences?

718. What do you know?

719. What are you trying to achieve (Objectives)?

720. Is the data sufficiently specified in terms of the type of failure being analyzed, and its frequency or probability?

721. What are your core values?

722. What will be the consequences if the risk happens?

723. What actions can be taken to eliminate or remove risk?

724. What are you here for (Mission)?

725. How reliable is the data source?

726. Whom do you serve (customers)?

727. What can happen?

728. Risk of what?

729. What are you weak at and therefore need to do better?

730. What is the chance that it will happen?

731. Who has a vested interest in how you perform as your organization (our stakeholders)?

732. How can it happen?

2.36 Procurement Management Plan: OT operational technology

733. What types of contracts will be used?

734. Have OT operational technology project management standards and procedures been identified / established and documented?

735. Is the steering committee active in OT operational technology project oversight?

736. Similar OT operational technology projects?

737. What are things that you need to improve?

738. Are updated OT operational technology project time & resource estimates reasonable based on the current OT operational technology project stage?

739. Are tasks tracked by hours?

740. What areas does the group agree are the biggest success on the OT operational technology project?

741. How will the duration of the OT operational technology project influence your decisions?

742. Does the OT operational technology project have a Statement of Work?

743. Are adequate resources provided for the quality assurance function?

744. Is the schedule updated on a periodic basis?

745. How and when do you enter into OT operational technology project Procurement Management?

746. Is OT operational technology project work proceeding in accordance with the original OT operational technology project schedule?

747. Is there an approved case?

2.37 Source Selection Criteria: OT operational technology

748. How organization are proposed quotes/prices?

749. In order of importance, which evaluation criteria are the most critical to the determination of your overall rating?

750. How do you consolidate reviews and analysis of evaluators?

751. How can solicitation Schedules be improved to yield more effective price competition?

752. What are the guiding principles for developing an evaluation report?

753. Do you have a plan to document consensus results including disposition of any disagreement by individual evaluators?

754. When should debriefings be held and how should they be scheduled?

755. Do you want to have them collaborate at subfactor level?

756. What will you use to capture evaluation and subsequent documentation?

757. What documentation should be used to support the selection decision?

758. What instructions should be provided regarding oral presentations?

759. What should clarifications include?

760. Is there collaboration among your evaluators?

761. How should the solicitation aspects regarding past performance be structured?

762. How will you decide an evaluators write up is sufficient?

763. When and what information can be considered with offerors regarding past performance?

764. How do you encourage efficiency and consistency?

765. How do you facilitate evaluation against published criteria?

766. How much past performance information should be requested?

767. Are responses to considerations adequate?

2.38 Stakeholder Management Plan: OT operational technology

768. Are you meeting your customers expectations consistently?

769. Are all payments made according to the contract(s)?

770. Has a quality assurance plan been developed for the OT operational technology project?

771. Is it standard practice to formally commit stakeholders to the OT operational technology project via agreements?

772. Does this include subcontracted development?

773. Describe the process that will be used to design, develop, review, accept, distribute and change outputs. Will all outputs delivered by the OT operational technology project follow the same process?

774. Are multiple estimation methods being employed?

775. Is the process working, and are people executing in compliance of the process?

776. Does the business case include how the OT operational technology project aligns with your organizations strategic goals & objectives?

777. Who is accountable for the achievement of the targeted outcome(s) and reports on the progress towards the target?

778. What is the process for purchases that arent acceptable (eg damaged goods)?

779. Can the requirements be traced to the appropriate components of the solution, as well as test scripts?

780. Are non-critical path items updated and agreed upon with the teams?

781. Has a structured approach been used to break work effort into manageable components (WBS)?

782. Why would a customer be interested in a particular product or service?

783. Are the people assigned to the OT operational technology project sufficiently qualified?

784. Is stakeholder involvement adequate?

2.39 Change Management Plan: OT operational technology

785. Who will be the change levers?

786. Why is it important?

787. What will be the preferred method of delivery?

788. What are you trying to achieve as a result of communication?

789. What provokes organizational change?

790. What are the essentials of the message?

791. How might they respond to the message and if the response may be negative or open to misinterpretation, what else needs to be said?

792. Has a training need analysis been carried out?

793. Has the training co-ordinator been provided with the training details and put in place the necessary arrangements?

794. Are there resource implications for your communications strategy?

795. Have the approved procedures and policies been published?

796. How badly can information be misinterpreted?

797. How much OT operational technology project management is needed?

798. Who might present the most resistance?

799. Are there any restrictions on who can receive the communications?

800. What is the most positive interpretation it can receive?

801. What relationships will change?

802. What are the specific target groups/audiences that will be impacted by this change?

803. What processes are in place to manage knowledge about the OT operational technology project?

3.0 Executing Process Group: OT operational technology

804. How well did the chosen processes fit the needs of the OT operational technology project?

805. How well defined and documented were the OT operational technology project management processes you chose to use?

806. How can software assist in procuring goods and services?

807. How do you measure difficulty?

808. Who are the OT operational technology project stakeholders?

809. What is the difference between conceptual, application, and evaluative questions?

810. Is the OT operational technology project making progress in helping to achieve the set results?

811. On which process should team members spend the most time?

812. How do you prevent staff are just doing busywork to pass the time?

813. What are the OT operational technology project management deliverables of each process group?

814. What were things that you did well, and could improve, and how?

815. What is the critical path for this OT operational technology project and how long is it?

816. How can you use Microsoft OT operational technology project and Excel to assist in OT operational technology project risk management?

817. Will outside resources be needed to help?

818. Why do you need a good WBS to use OT operational technology project management software?

819. How well did the team follow the chosen processes?

820. Do the products created live up to the necessary quality?

821. If a risk event occurs, what will you do?

3.1 Team Member Status Report: OT operational technology

822. What is to be done?

823. Do you have an Enterprise OT operational technology project Management Office (EPMO)?

824. Are the attitudes of staff regarding OT operational technology project work improving?

825. Are your organizations OT operational technology projects more successful over time?

826. How does this product, good, or service meet the needs of the OT operational technology project and your organization as a whole?

827. Is there evidence that staff is taking a more professional approach toward management of your organizations OT operational technology projects?

828. The problem with Reward & Recognition Programs is that the truly deserving people all too often get left out. How can you make it practical?

829. Will the staff do training or is that done by a third party?

830. How can you make it practical?

831. How much risk is involved?

832. How will resource planning be done?

833. Does your organization have the means (staff, money, contract, etc.) to produce or to acquire the product, good, or service?

834. Why is it to be done?

835. Does every department have to have a OT operational technology project Manager on staff?

836. Are the products of your organizations OT operational technology projects meeting customers objectives?

837. What specific interest groups do you have in place?

838. How it is to be done?

839. Does the product, good, or service already exist within your organization?

840. When a teams productivity and success depend on collaboration and the efficient flow of information, what generally fails them?

3.2 Change Request: OT operational technology

841. When to submit a change request?

842. What are the basic mechanics of the Change Advisory Board (CAB)?

843. Can you answer what happened, who did it, when did it happen, and what else will be affected?

844. Change request coordination ?

845. Is it feasible to use requirements attributes as predictors of reliability?

846. Since there are no change requests in your OT operational technology project at this point, what must you have before you begin?

847. What needs to be communicated?

848. Will there be a change request form in use?

849. Will all change requests be unconditionally tracked through this process?

850. What are the requirements for urgent changes?

851. Which requirements attributes affect the risk to reliability the most?

852. How many lines of code must be changed to

implement the change?

853. What type of changes does change control take into account?

854. Can static requirements change attributes like the size of the change be used to predict reliability in execution?

855. Who has responsibility for approving and ranking changes?

856. How is the change documented (format, content, storage)?

857. Who needs to approve change requests?

858. When do you create a change request?

859. What is the relationship between requirements attributes and attributes like complexity and size?

860. Will all change requests and current status be logged?

3.3 Change Log: OT operational technology

861. Does the suggested change request seem to represent a necessary enhancement to the product?

862. Is the change request within OT operational technology project scope?

863. Is the submitted change a new change or a modification of a previously approved change?

864. Is this a mandatory replacement?

865. How does this relate to the standards developed for specific business processes?

866. When was the request submitted?

867. Is the change request open, closed or pending?

868. How does this change affect scope?

869. Do the described changes impact on the integrity or security of the system?

870. Is the requested change request a result of changes in other OT operational technology project(s)?

871. Will the OT operational technology project fail if the change request is not executed?

872. Does the suggested change request represent a desired enhancement to the products functionality?

873. Is the change backward compatible without limitations?

874. Who initiated the change request?

875. When was the request approved?

876. How does this change affect the timeline of the schedule?

3.4 Decision Log: OT operational technology

877. How effective is maintaining the log at facilitating organizational learning?

878. What is the line where eDiscovery ends and document review begins?

879. At what point in time does loss become unacceptable?

880. What eDiscovery problem or issue did your organization set out to fix or make better?

881. How consolidated and comprehensive a story can you tell by capturing currently available incident data in a central location and through a log of key decisions during an incident?

882. Linked to original objective?

883. With whom was the decision shared or considered?

884. Behaviors; what are guidelines that the team has identified that will assist them with getting the most out of team meetings?

885. Do strategies and tactics aimed at less than full control reduce the costs of management or simply shift the cost burden?

886. How does an increasing emphasis on cost containment influence the strategies and tactics used?

887. Is your opponent open to a non-traditional workflow, or will it likely challenge anything you do?

888. Meeting purpose; why does this team meet?

889. Which variables make a critical difference?

890. What is your overall strategy for quality control / quality assurance procedures?

891. Adversarial environment. is your opponent open to a non-traditional workflow, or will it likely challenge anything you do?

892. How do you know when you are achieving it?

893. What is the average size of your matters in an applicable measurement?

894. What was the rationale for the decision?

895. Who will be given a copy of this document and where will it be kept?

896. How does the use a Decision Support System influence the strategies/tactics or costs?

3.5 Quality Audit: OT operational technology

897. Are there appropriate means for intervening if necessary?

898. How does your organization know that its systems for assisting staff with career planning and employment placements are appropriately effective and constructive?

899. For each device to be reconditioned, are device specifications, such as appropriate engineering drawings, component specifications and software specifications, maintained?

900. Are all records associated with the reconditioning of a device maintained for a minimum of two years after the sale or disposal of the last device within a lot of merchandise?

901. Will the evidence likely be sufficient and appropriate?

902. Are all employees including salespersons made aware that they must report all complaints received from any source for inclusion in the complaint handling system?

903. How does your organization know that its policy management system is appropriately effective and constructive?

904. How does your organization know that the review processes are effective?

905. Is your organizations resource allocation system properly aligned with its collection of intentions?

906. How does your organization know that its information technology system is serving its needs as effectively and constructively as is appropriate?

907. How does your organization know that its system for supporting staff research capability is appropriately effective and constructive?

908. Is your organizational structure established and each positions responsibility defined?

909. How does your organization know that its system for commercializing research outputs is appropriately effective and constructive?

910. How does your organization know that it provides a safe and healthy environment?

911. Are the policies and processes, as set out in the Quality Audit Manual, properly applied?

912. Are the review comments incorporated?

913. What are you trying to accomplish with this audit?

914. How does your organization know that its system for examining work done is appropriately effective and constructive?

915. Is progress against the intentions measurable?

916. What are the main things that hinder your ability to do a good job?

3.6 Team Directory: OT operational technology

917. Process decisions: how well was task order work performed?

918. How will the team handle changes?

919. Who are the Team Members?

920. Is construction on schedule?

921. Who are your stakeholders (customers, sponsors, end users, team members)?

922. Who should receive information (all stakeholders)?

923. Who will write the meeting minutes and distribute?

924. Process decisions: do job conditions warrant additional actions to collect job information and document on-site activity?

925. Who will be the stakeholders on your next OT operational technology project?

926. Where should the information be distributed?

927. How and in what format should information be presented?

928. Who will talk to the customer?

929. Process decisions: are all start-up, turn over and close out requirements of the contract satisfied?

930. Process decisions: are there any statutory or regulatory issues relevant to the timely execution of work?

931. Process decisions: which organizational elements and which individuals will be assigned management functions?

932. Decisions: is the most suitable form of contract being used?

933. How will you accomplish and manage the objectives?

934. How does the team resolve conflicts and ensure tasks are completed?

935. Why is the work necessary?

3.7 Team Operating Agreement: OT operational technology

936. What is your unique contribution to your organization?

937. Do you post meeting notes and the recording (if used) and notify participants?

938. The method to be used in the decision making process; Will it be consensus, majority rule, or the supervisor having the final say?

939. What resources can be provided for the team in terms of equipment, space, time for training, protected time and space for meetings, and travel allowances?

940. Did you draft the meeting agenda?

941. What are the safety issues/risks that need to be addressed and/or that the team needs to consider?

942. Do you call or email participants to ensure understanding, follow-through and commitment to the meeting outcomes?

943. What are some potential sources of conflict among team members?

944. Do you solicit member feedback about meetings and what would make them better?

945. Do you leverage technology engagement tools group chat, polls, screen sharing, etc.?

946. To whom do you deliver your services?

947. Did you delegate tasks such as taking meeting minutes, presenting a topic and soliciting input?

948. Reimbursements: how will the team members be reimbursed for expenses and time commitments?

949. Did you prepare participants for the next meeting?

950. Methodologies: how will key team processes be implemented, such as training, research, work deliverable production, review and approval processes, knowledge management, and meeting procedures?

951. Do you brief absent members after they view meeting notes or listen to a recording?

952. Confidentiality: how will confidential information be handled?

953. What types of accommodations will be formulated and put in place for sustaining the team?

954. Do you ask participants to close laptops and place mobile devices on silent on the table while the meeting is in progress?

3.8 Team Performance Assessment: OT operational technology

955. How much interpersonal friction is there in your team?

956. To what degree will the approach capitalize on and enhance the skills of all team members in a manner that takes into consideration other demands on members of the team?

957. What do you think is the most constructive thing that could be done now to resolve considerations and disputes about method variance?

958. To what degree does the teams work approach provide opportunity for members to engage in results-based evaluation?

959. To what degree can the team ensure that all members are individually and jointly accountable for the teams purpose, goals, approach, and work-products?

960. To what degree can all members engage in open and interactive considerations?

961. To what degree do team members agree with the goals, relative importance, and the ways in which achievement will be measured?

962. To what degree is the team cognizant of small wins to be celebrated along the way?

963. To what degree will the team ensure that all members equitably share the work essential to the success of the team?

964. To what degree is there a sense that only the team can succeed?

965. To what degree do team members feel that the purpose of the team is important, if not exciting?

966. To what degree are the goals realistic?

967. Where to from here?

968. How do you keep key people outside the group informed about its accomplishments?

969. If you have criticized someones work for method variance in your role as reviewer, what was the circumstance?

970. To what degree can team members frequently and easily communicate with one another?

971. Do friends perform better than acquaintances?

972. When does the medium matter?

973. Can familiarity breed backup?

974. How does OT operational technology project termination impact OT operational technology project team members?

3.9 Team Member Performance Assessment: OT operational technology

975. Why were corresponding selected?

976. What are top priorities?

977. What future plans (e.g., modifications) do you have for your program?

978. What, if any, steps are available for employees who feel they have been unfairly or inaccurately rated?

979. What specific plans do you have for developing effective cross-platform assessments in a blended learning environment?

980. What are best practices for delivering and developing training evaluations to maximize the benefits of leveraging emerging technologies?

981. How is your organizations Strategic Management System tied to performance measurement?

982. Can your organization rate by exception and assume that most employees are performing at an acceptable level?

983. Who they are?

984. Who is responsible?

985. For what period of time is a member rated?

986. What is the Business Management Oversight Process?

987. How are evaluation results utilized?

988. Did training work?

989. How do you make use of research?

990. How do you create a self-sustaining capacity for a collaborative culture?

991. What is the role of the Reviewer?

992. To what degree are the skill areas critical to team performance present?

993. How effective is training that is delivered through technology-based platforms?

994. How is the timing of assessments organized (e.g., pre/post-test, single point during training, multiple reassessment during training)?

3.10 Issue Log: OT operational technology

995. Is the issue log kept in a safe place?

996. Is access to the Issue Log controlled?

997. Where do team members get information?

998. Which stakeholders are thought leaders, influences, or early adopters?

999. What is the impact on the risks?

1000. Do you often overlook a key stakeholder or stakeholder group?

1001. Who needs to know and how much?

1002. In classifying stakeholders, which approach to do so are you using?

1003. Who reported the issue?

1004. Who have you worked with in past, similar initiatives?

1005. What is the impact on the Business Case?

1006. Persistence; will users learn a work around or will they be bothered every time?

1007. Can you think of other people who might have

concerns or interests?

1008. Are they needed?

4.0 Monitoring and Controlling Process Group: OT operational technology

1009. What areas were overlooked on this OT operational technology project?

1010. Is it what was agreed upon?

1011. Contingency planning. if a risk event occurs, what will you do?

1012. Where is the Risk in the OT operational technology project?

1013. Propriety: who needs to be involved in the evaluation to be ethical?

1014. What kinds of things in particular are you looking for data on?

1015. Accuracy: what design will lead to accurate information?

1016. Specific - is the objective clear in terms of what, how, when, and where the situation will be changed?

1017. How well did the chosen processes produce the expected results?

1018. How can you monitor progress?

1019. How was the program set-up initiated?

1020. Did you implement the program as designed?

1021. What are the goals of the program?

1022. What is the expected monetary value of the OT operational technology project?

1023. How are you doing?

1024. Feasibility: how much money, time, and effort can you put into this?

1025. Change, where should you look for problems?

4.1 Project Performance Report: OT operational technology

1026. To what degree does the teams purpose contain themes that are particularly meaningful and memorable?

1027. To what degree does the teams approach to its work allow for modification and improvement over time?

1028. To what degree does the information network communicate information relevant to the task?

1029. To what degree can team members meet frequently enough to accomplish the teams ends?

1030. To what degree are the tasks requirements reflected in the flow and storage of information?

1031. To what degree do members articulate the goals beyond the team membership?

1032. To what degree does the team possess adequate membership to achieve its ends?

1033. To what degree do the structures of the formal organization motivate taskrelevant behavior and facilitate task completion?

1034. How is the data used?

1035. What is the degree to which rules govern

information exchange between individuals within your organization?

1036. To what degree does the teams work approach provide opportunity for members to engage in open interaction?

1037. To what degree will each member have the opportunity to advance his or her professional skills in all three of the above categories while contributing to the accomplishment of the teams purpose and goals?

1038. To what degree will the team adopt a concrete, clearly understood, and agreed-upon approach that will result in achievement of the teams goals?

1039. To what degree does the information network provide individuals with the information they require?

1040. To what degree are the structures of the formal organization consistent with the behaviors in the informal organization?

1041. To what degree is there centralized control of information sharing?

1042. To what degree does the teams purpose constitute a broader, deeper aspiration than just accomplishing short-term goals?

4.2 Variance Analysis: OT operational technology

1043. Is all contract work included in the CWBS?

1044. What is your organizations rationale for sharing expenses and services between business segments?

1045. Why do variances exist?

1046. What types of services and expense are shared between business segments?

1047. Are your organizations and items of cost assigned to each pool identified?

1048. What is the dollar amount of the fluctuation?

1049. Contract line items and end items?

1050. Who are responsible for the establishment of budgets and assignment of resources for overhead performance?

1051. What does a favorable labor efficiency variance mean?

1052. There are detailed schedules which support control account and work package start and completion dates/events?

1053. What is the actual cost of work performed?

1054. How do you identify potential or actual overruns and underruns?

1055. Are the bases and rates for allocating costs from each indirect pool consistently applied?

1056. Are management actions taken to reduce indirect costs when there are significant adverse variances?

1057. At what point should variances be isolated and brought to the attention of the management?

1058. Are the wbs and organizational levels for application of the OT operational technology projected overhead costs identified?

1059. Are procedures for variance analysis documented and consistently applied at the control account level and selected WBS and organizational levels at least monthly as a routine task?

1060. Are there knowledgeable OT operational technology projections of future performance?

4.3 Earned Value Status: OT operational technology

1061. When is it going to finish?

1062. Earned value can be used in almost any OT operational technology project situation and in almost any OT operational technology project environment. it may be used on large OT operational technology projects, medium sized OT operational technology projects, tiny OT operational technology projects (in cut-down form), complex and simple OT operational technology projects and in any market sector. some people, of course, know all about earned value, they have used it for years - but perhaps not as effectively as they could have?

1063. Where is evidence-based earned value in your organization reported?

1064. How much is it going to cost by the finish?

1065. How does this compare with other OT operational technology projects?

1066. Where are your problem areas?

1067. Are you hitting your OT operational technology projects targets?

1068. Validation is a process of ensuring that the developed system will actually achieve the stakeholders desired outcomes; Are you building the right product? What do you validate?

1069. What is the unit of forecast value?

1070. Verification is a process of ensuring that the developed system satisfies the stakeholders agreements and specifications; Are you building the product right? What do you verify?

1071. If earned value management (EVM) is so good in determining the true status of a OT operational technology project and OT operational technology project its completion, why is it that hardly any one uses it in information systems related OT operational technology projects?

4.4 Risk Audit: OT operational technology

1072. Have permissions or required permits to use facilities managed by other parties been obtained?

1073. Are audit program plans risk-adjusted?

1074. What is happening in other jurisdictions? Could that happen here?

1075. Is the auditor truly independent?

1076. Is all required equipment available?

1077. What are the differences and similarities between strategic and operational risks in your organization?

1078. Does your organization have an up-to-date constitution?

1079. Does the customer have a solid idea of what is required?

1080. Is OT operational technology project scope stable?

1081. Is the auditor able to evaluate contradictory evidence in an unbiased manner?

1082. Are requirements fully understood by the team and customers?

1083. Do you have a mechanism for managing change?

1084. Are your rules, by-laws and practices non-discriminatory?

1085. Are tool mentors available?

1086. What compliance systems do you have in place to address quality, errors, and outcomes?

1087. Who audits the auditor?

1088. Does the customer understand the process?

1089. What responsibilities for quality, errors, and outcomes have been delegated to staff (or others) without adequate oversight?

4.5 Contractor Status Report: OT operational technology

1090. What are the minimum and optimal bandwidth requirements for the proposed solution?

1091. How is risk transferred?

1092. What was the overall budget or estimated cost?

1093. How long have you been using the services?

1094. If applicable; describe your standard schedule for new software version releases. Are new software version releases included in the standard maintenance plan?

1095. What is the average response time for answering a support call?

1096. What was the actual budget or estimated cost for your organizations services?

1097. Are there contractual transfer concerns?

1098. Describe how often regular updates are made to the proposed solution. Are corresponding regular updates included in the standard maintenance plan?

1099. What process manages the contracts?

1100. What was the final actual cost?

1101. How does the proposed individual meet each requirement?

1102. Who can list a OT operational technology project as organization experience, your organization or a previous employee of your organization?

1103. What was the budget or estimated cost for your organizations services?

4.6 Formal Acceptance: OT operational technology

1104. Was the OT operational technology project goal achieved?

1105. Is formal acceptance of the OT operational technology project product documented and distributed?

1106. Do you perform formal acceptance or burn-in tests?

1107. Who would use it?

1108. Was the client satisfied with the OT operational technology project results?

1109. How does your team plan to obtain formal acceptance on your OT operational technology project?

1110. Does it do what OT operational technology project team said it would?

1111. What is the Acceptance Management Process?

1112. What features, practices, and processes proved to be strengths or weaknesses?

1113. How well did the team follow the methodology?

1114. Was the sponsor/customer satisfied?

1115. Was business value realized?

1116. Did the OT operational technology project achieve its MOV?

1117. Does it do what client said it would?

1118. Was the OT operational technology project managed well?

1119. What was done right?

1120. What are the requirements against which to test, Who will execute?

1121. Have all comments been addressed?

1122. Who supplies data?

1123. Was the OT operational technology project work done on time, within budget, and according to specification?

5.0 Closing Process Group: OT operational technology

1124. Is this an updated OT operational technology project Proposal Document?

1125. Did you do what you said you were going to do?

1126. What were things that you did very well and want to do the same again on the next OT operational technology project?

1127. Based on your OT operational technology project communication management plan, what worked well?

1128. Did you do things well?

1129. Is the OT operational technology project funded?

1130. Who are the OT operational technology project stakeholders?

1131. Just how important is your work to the overall success of the OT operational technology project?

1132. Is this a follow-on to a previous OT operational technology project?

1133. How well did you do?

1134. What were the desired outcomes?

1135. What areas were overlooked on this OT operational technology project?

1136. Were sponsors and decision makers available when needed outside regularly scheduled meetings?

1137. Did the OT operational technology project team have enough people to execute the OT operational technology project plan?

1138. Is this a follow-on to a previous OT operational technology project?

5.1 Procurement Audit: OT operational technology

1139. Have late payment interests been rewarded and could they have been avoided?

1140. Are there authorizations on file to support all deductions from payroll checks?

1141. Are procurement processes well organized and documented?

1142. Were any additional works or deliveries admissible, without recourse to a new procurement procedure?

1143. Must the receipt of goods be approved prior to payment?

1144. Is there no evidence that the consultants participating in the OT operational technology project design released information to contractors competing for the prime contract?

1145. Do procedures require cash advances to be returned by transferred or terminated employees before they can receive final paychecks?

1146. Are cases of double payment duly prevented and corrected?

1147. Where your organization engaged an expert, was the contract awarded in compliance with procurement regulations?

1148. Did the contracting authority verify compliance with the basic requirements of the competition?

1149. Was the chosen procedure the most efficient and effective for the performance of the contract?

1150. When you set social or environmental conditions for the performance of the contract, were corresponding compatible with the law and was adequate information given to the candidates?

1151. Is an appropriated degree of standardization of goods and services respected?

1152. Does the procurement unit have sound commercial awareness and knowledge of suppliers and the market?

1153. Did the contracting authority offer unrestricted and full electronic access to the contract documents and any supplementary documents (specifying the internet address in the notice)?

1154. Was the decision on the award process accurate and adequately communicated?

1155. Is the efficiency of the procurement process regularly evaluated?

1156. Is the procurement OT operational technology project efficiently managed?

1157. Was confidentiality ensured when necessary?

1158. Were the specifications of the contract determined free from influence of particular interests of consultants, experts or other economic operators?

5.2 Contract Close-Out: OT operational technology

1159. Have all contracts been closed?

1160. Was the contract complete without requiring numerous changes and revisions?

1161. Has each contract been audited to verify acceptance and delivery?

1162. Change in circumstances?

1163. How/when used ?

1164. What is capture management?

1165. What happens to the recipient of services?

1166. Parties: Authorized?

1167. Are the signers the authorized officials?

1168. How does it work?

1169. Change in attitude or behavior?

1170. Have all contracts been completed?

1171. Have all acceptance criteria been met prior to final payment to contractors?

1172. Change in knowledge?

1173. Have all contract records been included in the OT operational technology project archives?

1174. Was the contract sufficiently clear so as not to result in numerous disputes and misunderstandings?

1175. How is the contracting office notified of the automatic contract close-out?

1176. Was the contract type appropriate?

1177. Parties: who is involved?

5.3 Project or Phase Close-Out: OT operational technology

1178. Does the lesson describe a function that would be done differently the next time?

1179. What was expected from each stakeholder?

1180. What is a Risk Management Process?

1181. Who controlled key decisions that were made?

1182. Were messages directly related to the release strategy or phases of the OT operational technology project?

1183. What was the preferred delivery mechanism?

1184. Did the OT operational technology project management methodology work?

1185. Can the lesson learned be replicated?

1186. What stakeholder group needs, expectations, and interests are being met by the OT operational technology project?

1187. What can you do better next time, and what specific actions can you take to improve?

1188. What are they?

1189. Planned remaining costs?

1190. What are the informational communication needs for each stakeholder?

1191. What information is each stakeholder group interested in?

1192. Did the delivered product meet the specified requirements and goals of the OT operational technology project?

1193. Were the outcomes different from the already stated planned?

1194. Was the schedule met?

1195. Planned completion date?

1196. What could have been improved?

5.4 Lessons Learned: OT operational technology

1197. What worked well/did not work well?

1198. How closely did deliverables match what was defined within the OT operational technology project Scope?

1199. Was there enough support – guidance, clerical support, training?

1200. How well is the build process working?

1201. What are the skills directly related to the task?

1202. What were the problems encountered in the OT operational technology project-functional area relationship, why, and how could they be fixed?

1203. How well prepared were you to receive OT operational technology project deliverables?

1204. What surprises did the team have to deal with?

1205. Is the lesson based on actual OT operational technology project experience rather than on independent research?

1206. What is the frequency of group communications?

1207. Who managed most of the communication

within the OT operational technology project?

1208. Would you spend your own time fixing this issue?

1209. What were the key issues?

1210. Who has execution authority?

1211. How much communication is socially oriented?

1212. What policy constraints are relevant?

1213. How effective was the support you received during implementation of the product/service?

1214. What are the performance measures?

1215. Was the purpose of the OT operational technology project, the end products and success criteria clearly defined and agreed at the start?

1216. How effective were the techniques used to prepare you and your organization for the impact of the changes brought about by the product or service produced by the OT operational technology project?

Index

ability 30, 79, 233
abnormal   191
abroad   140
absent 237
absorbed   208
absorption   209
accept   217
acceptable   59, 84, 102, 218, 240
acceptance   8, 129, 150, 154, 256, 263
accepted   113, 143
accepting   181
access 4, 10-12, 28, 77, 148, 155, 162, 199, 242, 261
accomplish   10, 83, 113, 122, 145, 232, 235, 246
accordance   180, 214
according   30, 39, 217, 257
account   35, 53, 155, 175, 226, 248-249
accounting   159
accounts   160
accuracy   60, 154, 244
accurate   12, 119, 149, 161, 244, 261
achievable   110
achieve   10, 70, 88, 92, 126, 165, 193-194, 211, 219, 221,
246, 250, 257
achieved   25, 88, 90, 115, 197, 256
achieving   230
acquire   224
acquired   163
across 58, 145, 190, 209
action 51, 58, 98-99, 106, 153, 181, 205
actionable   52, 110
actioned   146
actions 22, 58, 98, 105, 132, 193, 205, 211, 234, 249, 265
active 141, 213
actively   201
activities   19, 25, 27, 39, 85, 97, 102, 128, 141, 148, 162-166,
168-170, 176, 178, 180, 182-184, 197, 204-205
activity 5-6, 32, 34, 141-142, 163, 165, 167-171, 175-176, 178, 183-
184, 190, 199, 234
actual 34, 53, 187, 248-249, 254, 267
actually   41, 86, 106, 250

addition 112, 198
additional 31, 38, 71, 148, 185, 206, 234, 260
additions 97
address 1, 22, 86, 181, 193, 253, 261
addressed 141, 171, 202, 204, 236, 257
addressing 30, 122
adequate 41, 143, 145, 153, 213, 216, 218, 246, 253, 261
adequately 31, 159, 261
adjust 104
adjusted 104
admissible 260
adopters 242
advance 159, 247
advances 260
advantage 1, 70, 117
advantages 124, 168, 176
adverse 249
advise 2
Advisory 225
affect 65-66, 75, 127, 129, 142, 146, 151, 153, 156, 209, 225, 227-228
affected 140, 162, 175, 225
affecting 14, 27, 63
afford 205
affordable 84
against40, 103, 106, 160, 216, 233, 257
agencies 139
agenda 142, 236
agendas 125
agents 189
aggregate 58
agreed 147, 162, 218, 244, 268
Agreement 8, 122, 236
agreements 72, 85, 217, 251
agrees 126, 193
aiming 126
alerting 147
aligned 20, 232
aligns 161, 217
alleged 3
allocated 50, 59, 113, 159, 195
allocating 249
allocation 232

allowable   53
allowances   236
allowed   2, 123, 173
allows 12, 179
almost 250
already   110, 197, 224, 266
always 12
amended   190
Amongst   205
amount   19, 248
amplify70, 121
analvsis   203
analysis   4, 8, 12-13, 63-64, 71, 73, 79, 86, 89, 139, 143-144,
155, 161, 186-187, 191, 200, 207, 209-210, 215, 219, 248-249
analyze   4, 62, 73, 191
analyzed   79, 134, 146, 210-211
annual 160
another   165, 176, 239
answer 13-14, 18, 30, 47, 62, 78, 95, 108, 154, 225
answered   29, 45, 60, 77, 94, 107, 132
answering   13, 167, 254
anybody   141
anyone   37, 114, 128
anything   161, 171, 230
appear   3, 203
applicable   13, 95, 230, 254
applied   91, 103, 165, 206, 232, 249
appointed   31, 39
approach   47, 85, 91, 124, 218, 223, 238, 242, 246-247
approaches   92, 142, 201
approval   31, 128, 237
approvals   147-148, 155
approve   226
approved   44, 69, 134, 143, 147, 151, 187, 214, 219, 227-228,
260
approving   151, 226
architect   153
Architects   10
archives   264
around117, 139, 242
articulate   246
asking 3, 10, 126, 193-194
aspect 201

aspects   167, 216
aspiration   247
assess 19, 43, 79, 104, 119, 169
assessed   87, 146
assessing   81, 101
Assessment   7-8, 11-12, 24, 197, 203, 206-207, 238, 240
assets 59, 108
assign 22
assigned   144, 146, 153, 158, 162, 195, 200, 218, 235, 248
assigning   173
assignment   6, 195, 248
assist   11, 64, 82, 99, 185, 221-222, 229
assistant   10
assisting   231
associated   150, 209, 231
Assume   205, 240
assuming   207
Assumption   5, 155
assurance   28, 153, 162, 176, 182, 189, 200, 213, 217, 230
attached   178
attainable   33
attempted   37
attempting   96
attend 24
attendance   39
attendant   83
attended   1, 39
attention   14, 129, 249
attitude   263
attitudes   223
attributes   5, 111, 165, 225-226
audiences   220
audited   263
auditing   27, 97, 156, 159
auditor 252-253
auditors   189
audits 189, 253
author 3, 148
authority   68, 147, 197-198, 201, 261, 268
authorized   195, 263
automated   145
automatic   264

available   23, 28, 31, 40, 54, 66, 93, 99, 116, 163, 165, 179, 196, 207-208, 229, 240, 252-253, 259
Average   14, 29, 46, 60, 77, 94, 107, 132, 177, 230, 254
averse 208
avoided   260
awarded   260
awareness   261
background   12, 136, 168
backing   167
backup   239
backups   62
backward   228
balanced   85
bandwidth   254
barriers 117, 202
baseline   6, 123, 140, 143, 159, 187-188
baselined   200
baselines   31, 42
basics 131
because   2, 180
become   114-115, 119, 123, 147, 151, 229
becomes   209
before 1-2, 12, 37, 106, 145, 163, 169, 178, 200, 225, 260
beginning   4, 17, 29, 46, 61, 77, 94, 107, 132
begins 229
behavior   246, 263
behaviors   28, 47, 197, 229, 247
behind 2
belief   13, 18, 30, 47, 62, 78, 95, 108, 111
believable   110
believe2, 111, 126
Benchmark   191
benefit 3, 18, 20, 27, 59, 89, 98, 175
benefits   28, 48, 57, 59, 71, 108, 110, 115, 121-123, 150, 240
better 10, 37, 58, 82, 140, 177-178, 185, 204, 212, 229, 236, 239, 265
between   151, 155, 181, 202, 221, 226, 247-248, 252
beyond   246
biggest   89, 183, 213
blended   240
blinding   70
bother 55
bothered   242

bottleneck 178
bounce 65, 73
boundaries 38, 145
bounds 38
breakdown 5-6, 78, 142, 154, 157-158, 173
briefed 31
brings 36
broader 247
broken 74
brought 154, 249, 268
budget 2, 79, 103-104, 116, 146, 159, 179, 183, 187, 200, 254-255, 257
budgeted 53, 160, 195
budgets 26, 127, 159, 248
building 22, 99, 136, 142, 196, 250-251
burden 229
burn-in 256
business 2, 10, 12, 24, 28, 32, 44, 54, 59, 69, 72, 93, 106, 110, 113, 115, 121-122, 126, 128, 130, 136, 141, 148, 155, 161, 181, 203, 217, 227, 241-242, 248, 257
busywork 221
buy-in 119
buyout 144
by-laws 253
calculate 169, 176, 191
calculated 195
candidates 261
cannot 170, 179
capability 19, 155, 232
capable 10, 36
capacities 114
capacity 19, 22, 88, 241
capital 121
capitalize 74, 238
capture 52, 96, 191, 215, 263
captured 60, 68, 91, 128, 146, 181, 199-200
capturing 229
career 151, 198, 231
carried 77, 219
cash-flow 139
catching 1
categories 247
category 38

caused   3, 58
causes 50-51, 57, 62, 65, 69, 73, 105, 143
causing   27
celebrate   80
celebrated   238
center 60
central 229
centrally   85
certain 204
challenge   10, 230
challenges   116, 168
champions   194
chance   212
chances   204
change   7, 18-19, 44, 53, 69, 72-74, 76, 79, 85, 88-89, 103,
122, 138, 143, 147-148, 153-154, 158, 170, 179, 183, 187, 200, 203,
217, 219-220, 225-228, 245, 253, 263
changed   21, 44, 99, 127, 150, 186, 188, 225, 244
changes   21, 36, 45, 57, 69, 82-83, 87, 97, 106, 109, 127,
129, 134, 136, 153, 159-160, 162, 173, 176, 187, 189, 195-197, 225-
227, 234, 263, 268
changing   104, 117
chargeable   159
charged   58, 160
charter 4, 33, 43, 87, 136, 143, 182
charting   161
charts 68
cheaper   58
checked   63, 100-101, 105
checklists   11
checks 161, 260
choice 38, 130
choose   13, 91
chosen 137, 141, 210, 221-222, 244, 261
circumvent   27
claimed   3
claims 192
clarify 115
clearly 13, 18, 22, 30, 33, 38, 47, 62-63, 78, 85, 95, 108, 150, 198,
247, 268
clerical 267
client   114, 143, 256-257
clients 38

closed 102, 227, 263
closely 12, 267
Close-Out   8-9, 263-265
Closing8, 258
Coaches   40
coalitions   139
cognizant   238
colleague   127
colleagues   109, 124, 177
collect 71, 105, 186, 189, 193, 234
collected   37, 40, 67, 70, 73-74, 79
collection   64, 193, 232
coming   62
command   104
comments   232, 257
commercial   261
commit   203, 217
commitment 98, 109, 160, 236
committed   180-181, 208
committee   213
community   177, 185-186, 190
companies   3, 103
company   1-2, 10, 58, 70, 115, 119, 121, 126-129
compare   92, 250
compared   127, 145, 187
comparing   92
comparison   13
compatible   228, 261
compelling   42
competing   55, 260
competitor   2
complaint   231
complaints   192, 231
complete   3, 11, 13, 27, 31, 37, 43, 143, 154, 165, 169, 176-
178, 191, 198, 204, 263
completed   14, 32, 35, 40, 44, 145, 154, 163, 169, 200, 203,
235, 263
completely   1, 177
completing   131, 157
completion   32-33, 159, 246, 248, 251, 266
complex   10, 119, 155, 250
complexity   47, 66, 226

compliance   1, 20, 56-57, 59, 62, 85, 156, 190, 217, 253, 260-261
component   231
components   155, 218
compute   14
computer   155
concept   83, 154, 167, 193
concepts   155-156
conceptual   221
Concern   50, 198
concerned   19, 108
concerns   2, 24, 202, 243, 254
concrete   85, 187, 247
condition   99
conditions   101, 124, 234, 261
conduct   189
conducted   156, 187, 191
confidence   169, 192
confirm   13
conflict236
conflicts   149, 235
connected   129, 180
connecting   120
consensus   215, 236
consider   25, 27, 176, 236
considered   23-24, 54, 216, 229
considers   70
consistent   41, 55, 69, 101, 144, 195, 247
constantly   1
constitute   247
Constraint   5, 155
consult 1
consultant   1-2, 10
consulted   121, 202
consulting   2
consumers   127
contact   10, 146, 162
contacts   109
contain   23, 72, 102, 246
contained   3
contains   11
content   44, 143, 226
contents   3-4, 11

context   38-39, 41-42
continual   97, 102
continuous   70, 91
contract   8, 159-160, 170, 175, 183, 217, 224, 235, 248, 260-264
contracted   183
Contractor   8, 160, 175, 183, 254
contracts   31, 72, 213, 254, 263
contribute   149
control 4, 36, 53, 64, 79, 95-96, 98, 100-101, 103-105, 147, 153-154, 160, 162, 185, 226, 229-230, 247-249
controlled   71, 159, 242, 265
controls   23, 67, 81, 87, 96, 100, 103, 105, 170, 206
convention   111
conversion   155
convey   3
cooperate   186
Copyright   3
corporate   2
correct47, 95
corrected   260
corrective   58, 105
correctly   141
correspond   11-12
cosmetic   155
costing56
counter   139
counting   115, 163
counts 115
course 44, 53, 250
covering   11, 98, 198
covers 199
coworker   114
craziest   124
create 24, 75, 119, 121, 124, 154, 189, 226, 241
created   70, 76, 99, 138, 141, 161, 181, 222
creating   10
creative   29
creativity   80
credible   161, 186
crisis   21
criteria 4, 7, 11-12, 33, 38, 41, 75, 79, 81-82, 101, 121, 123, 133, 139, 150, 152, 186-187, 191, 215-216, 263, 268

CRITERION   4, 18, 30, 47, 62, 78, 95, 108
critical 35, 37, 44, 70, 80, 103, 113, 145, 155, 167-168, 178, 215,
222, 230, 241
criticism   76
criticized   239
Crosby 175
cross-sell   113
crucial 67, 167, 175
crystal 13
culture 36, 63, 142, 198, 241
current 34, 47, 51, 63, 73, 82, 104, 109, 111-112, 118, 121, 161,
170, 181, 194, 196, 206, 208, 213, 226
currently   30, 117, 229
custom 23
customer   28, 34-35, 37, 39-40, 88, 100, 104, 110, 116-117,
119, 127, 150, 203-204, 207-208, 218, 235, 252-253, 256
customers   3, 23, 32, 37, 51-52, 55, 63, 102, 108-110, 114, 116,
123, 125, 131, 156, 189, 203, 211, 217, 224, 234, 252
customized   2
cut-down   250
cutting 209
damage   3
damaged   218
Dashboard   11
dashboards   97
day-to-day   97, 120, 167
deadlines   23, 112
dealing   26
deceitful   114
decide 93, 197, 216
decided   91
deciding   131
decision   7, 49, 68, 79-81, 85, 89, 93, 134, 197, 215, 229-230,
236, 259, 261
decisions   80, 82, 84, 87, 90, 101-102, 135, 139, 197, 200,
213, 229, 234-235, 265
dedicated   10
deductions   260
deeper   13, 247
defective   209
define 4, 30, 36, 44-45, 66, 71, 78, 157, 175, 177, 191

defined   13, 18, 23, 25, 30-31, 33-35, 37-38, 41-42, 44-45, 47, 62, 67, 71, 78, 95, 108, 135, 146, 153-154, 158, 166, 188-189, 192, 197, 221, 232, 267-268

defines 28, 31, 39, 174

defining   10, 120, 137, 154

definite   102, 166

definition   18, 22, 35-36, 38, 44, 203

degree   180, 238-239, 241, 246-247, 261

-degree   2

delaying   58

delays 48, 177

delegate   237

delegated   36, 253

delete 183

deletions   97

deliver 23, 35, 88, 115, 117, 177, 185, 237

delivered   121, 147, 173, 179, 217, 241, 266

deliveries   260

delivering   240

delivers   174

delivery   21, 55, 118, 124, 209, 219, 263, 265

demand   121, 207, 210

demands   238

Deming   175

department   10, 121, 196, 224

depend   224

dependent   118, 148

depends   129

deploy 98, 116

deployed   100

deployment   57

derive 101

describe   24, 137, 151, 167, 217, 254, 265

described   3, 227

describing   32

deserving   223

design 12, 65, 76, 91-92, 104, 148, 156, 207, 210, 217, 244, 260

designated   181, 199

designed   10, 12, 71, 84-85, 245

designing   10

desired 28, 31, 69, 83, 173, 228, 250, 258

detail 47, 89, 137, 154, 165, 178

detailed   70, 75, 159, 163, 200, 248

details 53, 219
detect 101
determine 12, 112, 127, 141, 163, 176, 186, 190
determined 67, 127, 176, 193-194, 262
determines 183
detracting 126
develop 52, 78-79, 81, 86, 88, 144, 157, 217
developed 12, 42-44, 59, 82, 87, 148, 167, 200, 217, 227, 250-251
developer 204
developers 148
developing 65, 83, 215, 240
device 231
devices 237
diagram 5, 49, 51, 65, 169-170, 179
diagrams 55, 155, 161
dictates 180
Dictionary 5, 159
difference 141, 221, 230
different 10, 27, 35, 37, 39, 41, 64-65, 113, 127, 142, 155, 207, 266
difficult 164-166, 176
difficulty 221
dilemma 112
dimensions 21
direct 159, 196
direction 44, 58, 143
directly 3, 63, 139, 265, 267
Directory 8, 234
Disagree 13, 18, 30, 47, 62, 78, 95, 108
disaster 58, 96
disclosure 103
discussion 129
displayed 37, 69, 178
disposal 231
disputes 238, 264
disruptive 69
distribute 217, 234
Divided 29, 36, 45, 60, 77, 94, 107, 132
document 12, 34, 154, 182, 215, 229-230, 234, 258
documented 31, 83, 85, 96, 100, 102, 135, 147, 149, 153-156, 187, 190-191, 197-199, 213, 221, 226, 249, 256, 260
documents 10, 155, 261

dollar 248

domains   90

dormant   109

double 260

drawbacks   195

drawings   231

Driver 72

drivers 54, 72

drives 53

duplicate   190

duration   6, 141-142, 157, 175-177, 213

durations   34

during 44, 84, 144, 171, 184, 209, 229, 241, 268

dynamic   47

dynamics   43

eagerly   2

earlier 123

earliest 148

earned   8, 175, 195, 250-251

easily 239

economic   262

economical   112

Economy   79, 140

eDiscovery   229

edition 11

editorial   3

educated   1

education   102

effective   19, 21, 112, 115, 130, 178, 190, 215, 229, 231-232,
240-241, 261, 268

effects 49, 168

efficiency   72, 216, 248, 261

efficient   55, 89, 146, 224, 261

effort 34, 51, 55, 121, 160, 218, 245

efforts 37, 93, 139, 145, 200

electronic   3, 261

elements   12, 32, 67, 96, 127, 137, 154, 160, 175, 194-195,
235

eliminate   211

embarking   42

emergent   47

emerging   1, 68, 100, 240

emphasis   230

employed   176, 217
employee   93, 127, 255
employees   19, 23, 28, 70, 124-125, 129, 190, 231, 240, 260
employers   138
employment   231
empower   10
empowered   191
enable 69
enablers   118
encourage   80, 95, 216
energy 1
engage   112, 238, 247
engaged   260
engagement   52, 138, 201, 206, 237
enhance   98, 238
enhancing   97
enough   10, 69, 108, 116, 129, 134, 148-149, 151, 246, 259,
267
ensure 34, 40, 76, 83, 120, 123, 129-130, 141, 156, 194, 235-236,
238-239
ensured   261
ensures   120
ensuring   12, 113, 141, 250-251
entail   59
Enterprise   129, 223
entire   160, 180, 209
entities 59
entity   3
equipment   21, 27, 236, 252
equipped   40
equitably   36, 239
errors   128, 155, 253
escalated   183
Escalation   187
essence   137
essential   79, 239
essentials   120, 219
establish   78, 98, 185, 204
estimate   54, 59, 143, 177, 183-184
estimated   32-33, 54, 57, 183, 185, 254-255
estimates   6, 36, 48, 74, 146, 159, 175, 181-183, 187, 213
estimating   6, 145, 177, 181, 185, 200
estimation   81, 142, 217

estimator   183
etcetera   124
ethical 21, 119, 244
ethnic 121
evaluate   80, 83, 90, 159, 181, 252
evaluated   176, 261
evaluating   81-82
evaluation   75, 79, 88, 96, 191, 215-216, 238, 241, 244
evaluative   221
evaluators   215-216
events 24, 80, 87-88, 248
everyday   1, 70
everyone   36, 39, 193
everything   48
evidence   13, 51, 223, 231, 252, 260
evolution   47
evolve 102
examined   41
examining   232
example   4, 11, 15, 21, 67, 106, 143, 145, 160
examples   10-11, 176
exceed   157
exceeding   52
excellence   10, 35
exception   240
excessive   203
exchange   247
excited   1
exciting   239
exclude   82
execute   134, 257, 259
executed   187, 227
Executing   7, 217, 221
execution   98, 156, 175, 226, 235, 268
executive   10, 116
executives   113
exercise   26
existing 12, 106, 126, 148, 153
exists   148, 170
expect 113, 144, 178
expected   28, 34, 81, 123, 128, 141, 143, 176, 183, 244-245, 265
expense   248

expenses   237, 248
experience   34, 130, 168, 177, 197, 255, 267
experiment   123
expert 260
expertise   196, 208
experts 39, 175, 262
expiration   170
explained   12
explicitly   111
explore   65
export 139
exposure   206
extensive   2
extent 13, 19, 27, 41, 141, 160, 210
external   1-2, 37, 60, 191, 202
facilitate   13, 21, 75, 97, 216, 246
facilities   149, 252
facing 27, 112, 208
factors 51, 84, 126, 185, 209
failure 52, 120, 131, 211
fairly   36
familiar 11
fashion 3, 203
favorable   248
feasible   59, 70, 118, 185, 225
feature 12
features   143, 256
feedback   34, 40, 236
feeling 1
finalized   15
financial   52, 69, 71, 74, 117, 160, 167, 205
fingertips   12
finish   136, 148, 161, 163-165, 168, 170, 250
finished   136, 167
fixing   268
flexible 56
focused   47, 56, 60
follow   100, 120, 169-170, 217, 222, 256
followed   34, 145-146
following   11, 13, 154, 194
follow-on   258-259
follow-up   60, 184
for--and   103

forecast   251
forecasts   161
forefront   125
foresee   168
forever 127
forget 12
formal 8, 119, 156, 182, 246-247, 256
formally   45, 134, 146, 159, 208, 217
format 12, 161, 226, 234
formats   205
formula   14, 130
Formulate   30
formulated   144, 237
forward   2, 125
foster   111, 131
framework   104, 121, 193-194
freaky 108
frequency   41, 97, 188, 193, 211, 267
frequent   153, 199
frequently   54-55, 239, 246
friction 238
friend 112, 122, 127
friends 2, 239
frontiers   84
fulfill   114
full-blown   54
full-scale   92
function   213, 265
functional   160
functions   45, 75, 110, 125, 146, 150, 173, 197, 235
funded258
funding   116, 128, 134, 146, 148, 159, 206
further 11, 206
future   10, 51, 97, 100, 129, 207, 209-210, 240, 249
gained2, 98, 105
gather 13, 32, 36, 38, 40-41, 43, 45, 47, 62-63, 76
gathered   40, 63-64, 67, 69, 74, 76
gathering   34, 38, 42, 149, 203
general   91, 165
generally   224
generate   69, 71
generated   75
generation   11, 64

generic   2
gestation   210
getting 2, 196, 202, 229
Global 79, 168
govern 114, 246
governance   25, 126
governing   202
graphics   27
graphs 11
greater   143
greatest   87
ground 71
grouped   166
groups 127, 162, 181, 220, 224
growth 70, 126
guarantee   81
guidance   267
guidelines   229
guiding   215
handle 171, 209, 234
handled   237
handling   231
happen   24, 205, 211-212, 225, 252
happened   144, 225
happening   211, 252
happens   10, 45, 49, 51, 116, 127, 186, 191, 205, 211, 263
hardest   54
hardly 251
hardware   155
having 236
health 114
healthy   232
hearing   121
helping   10, 221
higher 160
highest 19
high-level   35, 40
highlight   2, 197
Highly 71
high-tech   119
hijacking   130
hinder 155, 233
hiring   97

historical 186
history 164
hitters 68
hitting 250
holders 146
holiday 2
honest 119
Honestly 2
horizon 115
housed 148
humans 10
hypotheses 62
identified 3, 20, 22, 24, 28, 35, 39, 63, 73, 80, 84, 150, 156, 159, 162, 165, 181, 187, 189, 195, 197-199, 206, 213, 229, 248-249
identify 1, 12-13, 24, 26, 67-68, 154, 160, 168, 186, 249
ignore 20
ignoring 113
imbedded 105
impact 7, 36, 48, 51, 55, 59, 93, 115, 135, 142, 148, 150, 176, 187, 203, 205-207, 209, 227, 239, 242, 268
impacted 51, 153, 220
impacts 56, 178
implement 22, 76, 95, 148, 195, 226, 245
implicit 121
import 139
importance 215, 238
important 20, 28, 41, 63, 74, 110, 116, 118, 124, 130, 139, 141-142, 201, 219, 239, 258
improve 4, 12, 71, 78-80, 82, 84, 86-89, 91, 136, 174, 213, 222, 265
improved 2, 86, 88-89, 94, 104, 140, 215, 266
improving 92, 176, 223
inactive 183
inadequate 1
incentives 97
incident 229
include 28, 82, 161, 163, 199, 216-217
included 4, 10, 20, 48, 142, 150, 155, 161, 177, 185, 248, 254, 264
INCLUDES 12
including 19, 33, 39-40, 52, 72, 78, 96, 99, 106, 155, 215, 231
inclusion 231
increase 119, 155

increased   117
increasing   109, 230
incurred   49
incurring   160
in-depth   11, 13
indicate   99, 121
indicated   105
indicators   24, 56, 63-64, 66, 82, 99, 207, 209
indirect   58, 160, 249
indirectly   3
individual   48, 164, 190, 215, 255
industrial   126, 210
industry   1-2, 99, 124, 127, 181
influence   84, 120, 138, 197-198, 201, 213, 230, 262
influences   168, 242
informal   247
informed   109, 239
ingrained   101
inherent   119
in-house   2, 136
initial   38, 131
initially 37
initiated   185, 228, 244
Initiating   4, 129, 134
initiative   13, 190, 193-194
Innovate   78
innovation   50, 68, 72, 79, 96, 131, 167, 190
innovative   124, 177, 185
in-process   64
inputs   32, 35, 96, 136, 175
inside   25
insight 66, 71
insights 1-2, 11
inspired   119
Instead2, 109
insure   125
integrate   80, 105, 114
integrated   207
integrity   19, 130, 227
intended   3, 92-93, 189
INTENT 18, 30, 47, 62, 78, 95, 108
intention   3
intentions   232-233

interact 110
interest 125, 201, 212, 224
interested 218, 266
interests 19, 140, 243, 260, 262, 265
interfaces 155
interim 112
internal 1, 3, 37, 75, 120, 191, 202
internet 261
interpret 13
interview 1, 128
introduce 47, 205
introduced 153
inventory 184
invest 63
investing 2
investment 19, 68, 193-194, 208-209
investor 51
involve 140, 146
involved 20, 23, 37, 56, 67, 71, 75, 83, 127, 148-149, 181, 190, 199-200, 203, 223, 244, 264
involves 101
isolated 249
issues 20, 22, 25-26, 134-135, 139, 145-146, 150, 153, 171, 182-183, 189, 235-236, 268
iteration 146
iterative 149
itself 3, 24
jointly 238
justified 99
killer 124
knowledge 1-2, 12, 34, 37, 43, 94, 97-99, 102, 105, 109, 111, 123, 130, 190, 197-198, 220, 237, 261, 263
lacked 99
laptops 237
largely 73
larger 56
latest 11
leader 21, 63, 65, 82
leaders 39, 73, 75, 98, 116, 124, 189-190, 242
leadership 26, 31, 45, 79, 114, 116
learned 1, 9, 96, 128, 193, 265, 267
learning 96, 98-99, 229, 240
lesson 265, 267

lessons 9, 92, 96, 128, 193, 267
Leveling   165
levels   19, 31, 63, 82, 99-100, 114, 157, 160, 162, 207, 210, 249
leverage   43, 79, 96, 186, 237
leveraged   37
leveraging   240
levers   219
liability 3
licensed   3
lifecycle   55, 66, 207
Lifetime   12
likelihood   89, 92, 205, 211
likely   91, 104, 127, 176, 203, 205, 207, 209, 230-231
limitation   51
limited 12, 198
linear   149
Linked 31, 229
listed   194, 196
listen   110, 124, 237
little   2
locally 85
location   229
logged 226
logical 169, 171
logically   162
longer 1, 104
long-term   100, 117, 129
looked 1
looking 20, 244
losses   23, 45
lowest 160, 169
magnitude   83
maintain   95, 126, 130, 135
maintained   86, 159, 231
majority   236
makers 93, 106, 134, 259
making   21, 68, 82, 85, 89, 124, 193, 197, 221, 236
manage   38, 45, 50, 56, 60, 71, 76, 82, 87-88, 93, 109, 126,
143-144, 147, 151, 167, 180-181, 190, 202, 220, 235
manageable 33, 91, 218
managed   10, 42, 67, 72-73, 80, 86, 93, 97, 103, 252, 257,
261, 267

management 5-7, 11-12, 18-19, 28, 32, 40, 57, 67, 70-72, 74, 76, 79-80, 84-85, 90-91, 93-94, 109-110, 120, 135, 143-145, 147, 154, 159-162, 166, 173, 179, 181-182, 189-190, 193, 195, 199-201, 203-205, 208-209, 213-214, 217, 219-223, 229, 231, 235, 237, 240-241, 249, 251, 256, 258, 263, 265

manager   10, 12, 28, 32, 40, 123, 143, 147, 175, 181, 189, 224

managers   4, 133, 161, 208

manages   90, 254

managing   4, 83, 133, 138-139, 253

mandatory   227

manner   23, 84, 135, 146, 190, 195, 238, 252

mantle 130

Manual   232

Mapping   67, 72, 75

margin 162

marked   154

market 26, 205, 250, 261

marketable   205

marketer   10

marketing   127, 190

markets   27

material   160

materials   3

matrices   151

Matrix 4-7, 139, 151, 192, 195, 209

matter 39, 56, 239

matters   230

maturing   210

maximize   208, 240

maximizing   111, 175

meaningful   50, 120, 204, 246

measurable   33, 35, 183, 233

measure   4, 12, 21, 27, 43, 47-50, 52, 55-57, 62, 72, 78, 80, 88, 90, 96, 100, 103, 105, 140, 186, 194, 221

measured   28, 49, 51-52, 56, 59, 83, 96, 106, 238

measures   49-50, 52, 55-56, 58, 63-64, 72, 74, 82, 99, 268

measuring   97

mechanical   3

mechanics   225

mechanism   253, 265

mechanisms   153

mechanized   181

medium   239, 250
meeting   33, 42, 100, 146, 217, 224, 230, 234, 236-237
meetings   37, 39-40, 153, 229, 236, 259
megatrends   113
member   7-8, 31, 114, 223, 236, 240-241, 247
members   1, 34, 36, 40, 73, 99, 146, 182, 199-200, 202, 221, 234, 236-239, 242, 246-247
membership   246
memorable   246
Mentally   148
mentors   253
message   104, 219
messages   201, 265
method   60, 143, 177, 192, 201, 219, 236, 238-239
methods   34, 41, 59, 63, 154, 186, 207, 210, 217
metrics 6, 33, 76, 97, 146-147, 181, 191-192, 204
Microsoft   222
milestone   5, 145, 167
milestones   33, 138, 162, 165, 169
minimize   135, 142, 203
minimizing   66, 111
minimum   231, 254
minority   19
minutes   33, 80, 146, 234, 237
missed 56, 121
missing 65, 121, 165
mission 70, 75, 125, 130, 198, 211
Mitigate   85, 135, 142
mitigated   2, 204
mitigating   181
mitigation   143, 180-181, 208
mobile 237
Modeling   73, 194
models26, 48, 66, 112
modified   98
module   180
moment   115
moments   67
momentum   115, 121
Monday   1
monetary   18, 245
monitor   93, 96, 102, 105, 145, 186, 244
monitored   97, 103, 175

monitoring   8, 96-97, 99, 102-103, 161, 171, 207, 244
monthly   249
months 1, 80, 89
morning   1
motivate   125, 246
motivation   22, 106, 136
motive 193-194
movement   175
moving   125
multiple   217, 241
narrative   167, 190
narrow 73
nature 47, 160
nearest   14
nearly 126
necessary   66, 68, 74, 76, 92, 109, 112, 124, 141, 155, 186,
195, 204, 219, 222, 227, 231, 235, 261
needed   2, 20-23, 26, 35, 65, 74, 104-106, 136, 175, 178,
184, 193, 196, 202, 220, 222, 243, 259
negative   129, 139, 219
negotiate   114
negotiated   122
neither 3
nervous   148
network   5, 169-170, 179, 246-247
Neutral 13, 18, 30, 47, 62, 78, 95, 108
non-OT 148
normal 101
notice 3, 141, 261
notified   209, 264
notify   236
number   29, 45, 49, 60, 77, 94, 107, 132, 165, 190, 209, 269
numbers   129
numerous   263-264
objection   19
objective   10, 48, 136, 140, 229, 244
objectives   2, 20, 25, 28, 30-31, 42, 70, 75, 101, 106, 115, 117-
118, 121, 149, 161, 187, 189, 206, 211, 217, 224, 235
observe   197
observed   86
observing   156
obsolete   113
obstacles   27, 177, 185

obtain 110, 256
obtained   40, 155, 252
obviously   13
occurrence   209
occurring   85
occurs 21, 58, 106, 134, 176, 222, 244
offerings   92
offerors216
office   135, 154, 161, 189, 223, 264
Officer 1
officials263
onboarding   162
one-time   10
ongoing   84, 96
on-going   145-146
on-site 234
operates   124
operating   8, 48, 54, 101, 159, 236
operation   98, 178
operations   12, 97, 101, 106
operators   100, 262
opponent   230
opposed   201
opposite   111, 124
opposition   109
optimal   86, 89, 93, 254
optimize   85, 97
optimized   123
optimiztic   176
option 130
options28
ordered   1
organized   165, 241, 260
orient 100
oriented   268
original179-180, 187, 203, 214, 229
originate   106, 201
others 180, 185-186, 191, 195, 198, 201-202, 204-205, 253
otherwise   3
outcome   13, 81, 135, 139, 173, 207, 218
outcomes   81, 86, 97, 177, 185, 236, 250, 253, 258, 266
outlined   101
output 43, 63, 65-66, 68-70, 75, 77, 99, 101

outputs   32, 65, 69, 71, 76, 96, 153, 171, 175, 217, 232
outside 80, 222, 239, 259
Outsource   63, 136
outsourced   175
outweigh   57
overall 12-13, 20, 53, 106, 114, 122, 142, 149, 155, 169, 205, 215, 230, 254, 258
overcome   177, 185
overhead   159-160, 248-249
overheads   182
overlook   242
overlooked   134, 184, 199, 244, 259
overruns   249
oversight   76, 161, 213, 241, 253
overtime   171
owners 158
ownership   33, 102
package   248
packages   159, 195
paradigms   112
paragraph   124
parameters   103
Pareto 68, 161
particular   67, 218, 244, 262
Parties 2, 252, 263-264
partners   23, 37, 104, 116, 125, 129
pattern   165
patterns   88
paycheck   128
paychecks   260
paying 129
payment   146, 260, 263
payments   217
payroll 260
pending   227
people 10, 22, 50, 64, 76, 83, 90, 95, 101, 109-111, 113, 118, 121, 124, 134, 140, 162, 195, 200, 217-218, 223, 239, 242, 250, 259
perceive   129
percent   123
percentage   151
perception   78, 88, 119
perform   22, 30, 36, 161, 163, 173, 190, 209, 212, 239, 256
performed   84, 151, 160, 163-164, 195, 203, 234, 248

296

performing   134, 195, 240
perhaps   21, 250
period 84, 184, 210, 241
periodic   214
periods160
permission   3
permit 47
permits252
person 3, 20, 183
personal   120
personally   151
personnel   18, 29, 66, 170, 179, 193-194, 209
phases 55, 80, 165, 203, 265
phrase 148
pitfalls 119
placements   231
places 183
planet 101
planned   97, 100-101, 103, 159-161, 195, 205, 265-266
planners   106
planning   4, 11, 99, 106, 141, 144, 148, 169, 171, 224, 231,
244
platforms   241
players 90
playing2
pocket185
pockets   185
points 29, 45, 60, 68, 77, 94, 107, 132, 193
policies   139, 146, 219, 232
policy 42, 82, 106, 171, 231, 268
political   41, 114, 168, 209
population   141
portfolio   108
portion 2
portray68
positioned   185-186
positions   232
positive   89, 121, 129, 143, 201, 220
possess246
possible   50, 69, 73, 88, 95, 130, 177
post-test   241
potential   24, 51, 82-85, 113, 118, 131, 176, 202, 236, 249
practical   70, 78, 95, 223

practice   208, 217
practices   12, 66, 88, 96-97, 144, 240, 253, 256
precaution   3
predict 226
predicting   97
prediction   166
predictors   225
preferred   219, 265
pre-filled   11
prepare   198, 201, 237, 268
prepared   1, 129, 267
preparing   180
present   100, 110, 129, 220, 241
presented   1, 22, 176, 234
presenting   237
preserve   39
preserved   71
pressing   134
prevailing   210
prevent   53, 182, 221
prevented   260
prevents   21
previous   37, 255, 258-259
previously   227
prices 215
primary   59, 136
principles   215
priorities   54-55, 57-58, 240
Priority 58, 165
privacy   38
probably   174
problem   18, 21-22, 25-28, 30, 33, 37, 41, 52, 54, 70, 223,
229, 250
problems   22-27, 79, 81, 85, 105, 122, 139, 193-194, 245, 267
procedure   162, 260-261
procedures   12, 83, 96, 100-102, 145, 159, 171, 182, 188, 190-
191, 193, 213, 219, 230, 237, 249, 260
proceed   207
proceeding   178, 180, 214

process   4, 6-8, 10, 12, 32, 34-35, 40-43, 51, 63-76, 86, 91, 93, 97-102, 104, 106, 134, 141, 144-145, 147-149, 151, 153-154, 156, 162, 171, 177, 189-190, 193-194, 200, 203, 207-208, 217-218, 221, 225, 234-236, 241, 244, 250-251, 253-254, 256, 258, 261, 265, 267

processes   1, 53, 63-64, 66, 68-72, 74-76, 96-97, 106, 135, 139, 141, 145, 156, 194, 205, 220-222, 227, 232, 237, 244, 256, 260

procuring   221

produce   1, 68, 141, 171, 224, 244

produced   66, 89, 268

producing   151

product   3, 54, 63, 124, 128, 142, 146-147, 153, 167, 203, 205, 209, 218, 223-224, 227, 251, 256, 266, 268

production   37, 84, 117, 237

products   3, 21-22, 108, 120, 141, 151, 222, 224, 228, 268

program   21, 58, 72, 103, 141-142, 189, 198, 205, 240, 244-245, 252

Programs   223

progress   31, 51, 80, 106, 124, 129, 182, 186, 193, 218, 221, 233, 237, 244

project 4-6, 8-11, 22-24, 27, 43, 54, 66, 71, 75, 93, 97, 101, 103, 110, 113-114, 118-119, 123, 125, 128, 131, 133-149, 151, 153-154, 156-158, 161-167, 169-170, 173-182, 184-191, 196-201, 203, 205-210, 213-214, 217-218, 220-225, 227, 234, 239, 244-246, 250-252, 255-261, 264-268

projected   196, 249

projects   4, 57, 123, 131, 133, 141-142, 151, 157, 161, 176, 188, 197, 206, 213, 223-224, 250-251

promising   124

promote   76, 190

promptly   183

proofing   86

proper 103, 147

properly   34, 39, 208, 232

Proposal   167, 258

proposals   106

proposed   22, 57, 81, 85, 143, 149, 176, 215, 254-255

Propriety   244

protect   67, 113

protected   71, 236

protection   111

protocols   191

proved 256

provide   21, 66, 120, 128, 130, 134, 138, 143, 159, 161, 170, 177, 185, 238, 247
provided   2, 14, 99, 176, 199, 213, 216, 219, 236
provides   232
providing   103, 137-138, 154, 167
provokes   219
public 142
published   216, 219
publisher   3
pulled 123
purchase   10
purchases   218
purchasing   1-2
purpose   4, 12, 125, 173, 185, 193, 230, 238-239, 246-247, 268
pursuing   2
pushing   108
qualified   36, 64, 71, 73-74, 162, 200, 218
qualifies   65, 77
qualify 56, 69
qualities   20
quality 6, 8, 12, 28, 52, 58, 63, 70, 73, 80, 99, 101, 115, 141, 153, 161-162, 175-176, 182, 189, 191-194, 197-200, 213, 217, 222, 230-232, 253
quantified   101
quantify   56
question   13, 18, 30, 47, 62, 78, 95, 108, 117
questions   10-11, 13, 70, 154, 204, 221
quickly 12, 65, 67, 73
quotes 215
radically   69
raised 146
ranking226
rather 47, 109, 267
rating 215
rationale   230, 248
reached   21
reaching   115
reactivate   109
readiness   37
readings   105
realistic   21, 120, 179, 239
reality 161, 188, 209

realize 2, 54
realized   122, 257
realizing   1
really   10, 23, 41, 145, 195
reason 111, 116
reasonable   91, 121, 181-182, 213
reasons   42
re-assign   165
reassigned   188
rebuild 124
recast 183
receipt260
receive   11-12, 32, 52, 201, 220, 234, 260, 267
received   31, 110, 204, 231, 268
recently   116
recipient   27, 263
recognised   91
recognize   4, 18-21, 23, 25, 56, 80, 88
recognized   19, 22-25, 27-28, 69, 181
recognizes   28
recommend   112, 127
record 193
recording   3, 236-237
records   111, 159, 189, 231, 264
recourse   260
recovery   96, 179
redefine   21, 38
re-design   74
reduce205, 229, 249
reducing   100, 109
references   269
reflect 98, 103, 105, 161
reflected   246
reform 106, 109, 118
reforms22, 59
refreshed   2
regarding   120-121, 156, 189, 216, 223
Register   4, 7, 138, 205
regret 89
regular 31, 37, 62, 69, 153, 254
regularly   34, 39, 153, 259, 261
regulatory   20, 235
reimbursed   237

reject   147
relate   74, 227
related26, 63, 103, 153, 251, 265, 267
relation   27-28, 88, 125
relations   210
relative106, 238
relatively   119
release146, 162, 265
released   260
releases   254
relevant   33, 59, 66, 104, 127, 235, 246, 268
reliable40, 211
relieved   2
relocation   144
remain 32
remaining   186, 265
remember   177
remove   211
remunerate   93
rephrased   12
replace   60
replacing   148
replicate   190
replicated   265
Report 7-8, 87, 105, 182, 215, 223, 231, 246, 254
reported   153, 242, 250
reporting   70, 106, 114, 145, 147, 153, 159-160, 205
reports 2, 52, 105, 138, 147, 183, 199, 218
repository   199
represent   83, 227-228
reproduced   3
reputation   117
request   7, 70, 147, 187, 200, 225-228
requested   3, 82, 134, 187, 216, 227
requests   225-226
require 54, 66, 68, 98, 106, 137, 159, 171, 206, 247, 260
required   21, 26, 33-34, 37, 42-43, 53, 60, 66, 74, 81, 85, 93,
99, 134, 150, 163, 165, 177, 179, 197, 208, 252
requiring   138, 263
research   26, 117, 124, 232, 237, 241, 267
reserve159, 181
reserved   3
reserves   159, 181

reside 90
resistance   220
resolution   66, 80
resolve 18, 22, 26, 165, 235, 238
resolved   146, 183, 203
resource   5-6, 131, 142, 161, 165, 171, 173, 181, 199, 213,
219, 224, 232
resources   2, 4, 10, 21, 23, 27, 31, 40-41, 53, 69, 79, 93, 99,
105, 113, 131, 135, 144, 146, 153, 163, 165, 170, 173, 179, 186,
188, 213, 222, 236, 248
respect   3
respected   261
respond   219
responded   14
response   21, 26, 99-100, 102, 105, 176, 219, 254
responses   93, 129, 216
responsive   177, 185
result   83, 89, 142, 153, 183, 185, 187, 191, 219, 227, 247, 264
resulted   107
resulting   71, 143
results 11, 34-35, 56, 78, 80-81, 85-87, 92, 99, 141, 165, 179, 186,
207, 215, 221, 241, 244, 256
Retain 108
retained   64
retention   60
retrospect   123
return 89, 117, 193-194, 208
returned   260
returns 192
revenue   58
revenues   59
review 12, 37, 60, 71, 169, 189, 191, 217, 229, 232, 237
reviewed   42
Reviewer   239, 241
reviews153, 156, 169, 215
revised 74, 107
revisions   263
reward 48, 65, 223
rewarded   19, 260
rewards   97
rework 57
rights   3
routine 97, 249

safeguard 139
safety 120, 236
samples 189-190
sampling 161
sanitized 155
satisfied 121, 235, 256
satisfies 251
satisfying 112
savings 36, 49, 54, 74
scalable 92
scenario 39, 45
scenes 2
schedule 5-6, 30, 48, 78, 104, 116, 150, 160-162, 169-170, 175, 179-180, 182, 199, 214, 228, 234, 254, 266
scheduled 148, 189, 195, 215, 259
scheduler 181
schedules 161, 169, 179, 215, 248
scheduling 162, 181, 200
scheme 102
Science 72, 177
scientific 177
Scorecard 4, 14-16
scorecards 97
Scores 16
scoring 12
screen 237
scripts 218
seamless 125
second 14
secret 2
secrets 1
section 14, 29, 45-46, 60, 77, 94, 107, 132
sector 126, 250
securing 52, 111
security 27, 72, 89, 104-105, 138, 155, 191, 227
segmented 39
segments 37, 127, 248
select 74, 105
selected 86, 91, 144, 186, 240, 249
selecting 123
Selection 7, 215
self-help 2
seller 183

sellers 3
selling 119
senior 98, 110, 114, 116, 189-190
sensitive   43, 59
sequence   164, 169
sequenced   162
sequencing   118, 141
series 13
Service 1-4, 10, 54, 78, 88, 99, 124, 153, 167, 205, 218, 223-224, 268
services   3, 55, 108, 111, 130, 175, 183, 206, 221, 237, 248, 254-255, 261, 263
serving 232
session 148
setbacks   65, 73
setting 120
set-up 244
several 64
severely   74
shared 98, 186, 229, 248
sharing 94, 98, 146, 190, 237, 247-248
shifts   29
shopping   1
shorten 179
short-term   208, 247
should 10, 22-25, 35, 40-41, 52-53, 55, 63-64, 67, 72, 74, 79-80, 83, 91, 103, 112, 119, 121-122, 124-125, 132, 135-136, 138, 142-143, 163, 173, 180, 184, 187, 190, 198, 204-210, 215-216, 221, 234, 245, 249
signature   130
signatures   171
signers 263
silent   237
similar 37, 43, 68, 92, 164-165, 213, 242
simple 119, 250
simply 11, 229
single   124, 241
single-use   10
situation   2, 23, 47, 141, 205, 209, 244, 250
situations   104
skeptical   127
skills   19, 27, 68, 110-111, 123, 168, 197, 208, 238, 247, 267
smallest   27, 89

soccer 1
social   127, 261
socially 268
societal   114
software   21, 142, 145-147, 175, 190, 203, 207-208, 221-222,
231, 254
solicit   34, 236
soliciting   237
solution   1, 59, 66, 70, 78, 82-86, 89, 91-95, 153, 218, 254
solutions   54, 78, 82-83, 89, 92, 97, 206
solved 25
Someone   10
someones   239
something   126, 143
Sometimes   54
source 7, 109, 128, 211, 215, 231
sources   32, 65, 68, 236
special 43, 99, 137
specific   11, 24, 33, 35, 42, 68, 120, 148, 156, 164-166, 171,
176, 197, 207, 220, 224, 227, 240, 244, 265
specified   115, 160, 211, 266
specifying   261
spending   2
spoken 116
sponsor   28, 136, 146, 256
sponsors   23, 193, 234, 259
spread 95, 104
stable   252
staffed 31
staffing 19, 97, 143, 182
stages 144
standard   10, 99, 102, 172, 191, 217, 254
standards   12-13, 95, 98, 101, 105, 155, 190-191, 194, 213,
227
started 11, 167
starting 12
start-up   235
stated 111, 123, 197, 266
statement   5, 13, 79, 81, 136, 148, 153-154, 183, 213
statements   14, 29, 33, 45, 60, 77, 94, 107, 132
static   226
status 7-8, 76, 145, 153, 160-161, 182, 199, 206, 223, 226, 250-
251, 254

statutory   235
steady 49
steering   213
stopper   149
storage   226, 246
stories 32
strategic   54, 90, 106, 118, 161, 217, 240, 252
strategies   83, 104, 109, 180, 229-230
strategy   20, 36, 54, 59, 84, 87, 91, 99, 118, 122, 219, 230,
265
Stream 72, 75
strength   140
strengths   140, 155, 168, 256
strict   72
strong 197
Strongly   13, 18, 30, 47, 62, 78, 95, 108
structure   5-6, 53, 78, 93, 119, 126, 142, 154, 157-158, 160,
173, 232
structured   110, 216, 218
structures   246-247
stubborn   114
stupid 131
subfactor   215
subject 11-12, 39
subjects   71
submit 225
submitted   227
subsequent   215
subset 27
succeed   50, 129, 239
success   21, 25, 35, 37-38, 43, 50, 52, 56, 88-90, 106, 113,
117, 121, 124, 126, 130-131, 142, 181, 184, 191, 213, 224, 239,
258, 268
successes   109
successful   1, 70, 83, 98, 113, 118-119, 141, 174-175, 223
succession   106
sufficient   141, 216, 231
suggest   207
suggested   105, 227-228
suitable   235
summarized   160
Sunday   1
superior   1

supervisor   197, 236
supplier   90, 110
suppliers   32, 71, 77, 116, 261
supplies   257
supply 49, 111
support   3, 10, 21, 68, 92, 96, 98, 104, 109-110, 130, 135,
137, 145-146, 171, 181, 198, 206, 208, 215, 230, 248, 254, 260,
267-268
supported   63, 149
supporting   85, 103, 182, 190, 232
surface   105
surprises   267
SUSTAIN   4, 85, 108
sustaining   100, 237
symptom   18, 57
system 12, 42, 70, 96, 116, 147-150, 155-156, 159-160, 227, 230-
232, 240, 250-251
systematic   47, 57
systems   1, 47, 62, 65, 68, 70, 72, 74, 88, 97, 139, 145, 153,
175, 231, 251, 253
tables 155
tackle 57
tackled   139
tactics 229-230
Taguchi   175
tailored   2
takers 153
taking 58, 141, 204, 223, 237
talent 64, 114
talents 111
talking 10
tallied 187
tangle 196
target 32, 123, 141, 191, 218, 220
targeted   218
targets 183, 250
tasked 102
technical   155, 168, 175
techniques   66, 112, 134, 144, 176, 268
technology   1, 3-9, 11-16, 18-49, 51-61, 63-99, 101-107, 109-
149, 151, 153-159, 161-167, 169-171, 173-191, 193, 195-201, 203,
205-211, 213-215, 217-225, 227, 229, 231-232, 234, 236-240, 242,
244-246, 248-252, 254-261, 263-268

templates   10-11

terminated   260

testable   32

test-cycle   193

tested 25

testing 82, 86, 191, 210

themes246

themselves   1, 47, 118

theory 106

therefore   212

things 87, 125, 199, 203, 213, 222, 233, 244, 258

thinking   80

thorough   92, 187

thought   242

threat 25, 122

threats 1-2

through   69, 73, 116, 160, 207, 225, 229, 241

throughout   3, 66, 129, 169, 175

throughput   175

Thursday   1

tighter 127

time-bound   33

timeframe   73, 166, 186

timeframes   26

timeline   228

timely 23, 84, 135, 146, 195, 203, 235

timetable   169

timing 241

todays 175

together   124

tolerances   84

tolerate   204

tolerated   163

tomorrow   101, 128, 134

toolkit 1-2

toolkits 1-2

top-down   104

topics 199

toward 100, 223

towards   2, 66, 142, 218

traced 218

tracing 148

tracked   145, 213, 225

tracking   39, 106, 181
traction   127
trademark   3
trademarks   3
trade-offs   181
trained 39, 189-190
training   20-22, 66, 73, 80, 97, 99, 102, 198, 204, 219, 223, 236-237, 240-241, 267
trainings   26
Transfer   14, 29, 46, 61, 77, 94, 97, 102, 107, 132, 254
transition   123, 207
translated   35
travel 196, 236
trends 63, 68, 82, 129, 143
trigger 81, 84
triggers 91, 199
trophy 130
trouble 123
trying 10, 114, 130, 211, 219, 232
turnaround   166
unaware   1
unbiased   252
unclear   45
uncovered   2
underlying   79
undermine   114
underruns   249
understand   37, 76, 147-148, 180, 253
understood   91, 110, 203, 247, 252
undertake   66, 205
underway   82
unfairly 240
uninformed   109
unique 2, 119, 236
Unless 10
unprepared   1
unresolved   171
update   1
updated   11-12, 153, 169, 181-182, 213-214, 218, 258
updates   12, 97, 254
up-sell 113
up-to-date   252
urgent 225

usability   88, 132
useful 84, 101, 157, 204-205
usefully 12, 27
usually 1
utility   178
utilized 159, 241
utilizing 1, 93
validate   57, 251
validated   35, 40, 42, 75
Validation   250
valuable   10
values 98, 116, 211
variables   65, 101, 230
variance   8, 238-239, 248-249
variances   248-249
variation   18, 34, 65, 68, 100
variations   149
variety 90
vendor 85, 170
Vendors   22, 181
verified 12, 35, 40, 42, 75, 167
verify   49-55, 57-58, 60, 99-100, 154, 251, 261, 263
verifying   49-50, 56, 59, 153
Version 254, 269
versions   35, 41
vested 125, 212
viable 97, 157
violated   156
vision   116, 143, 198
visualize   178
voices 138, 140
volatile 79
vulnerable   111
waited 2
walking   2
warrant   234
warranty   3, 192
weaknesses   155, 256
weeknights   1
whether   10, 101, 131, 197
widespread   100
willing 203-204
window   166

within 1-2, 66, 84, 224, 227, 231, 247, 257, 267-268
without1, 3, 14, 124, 126, 150, 207, 228, 253, 260, 263
worked   144, 203, 242, 258, 267
workers   121
workflow   67, 230
workforce   19, 82, 112, 116, 127
working   2, 93, 100-101, 179, 217, 267
Worksheet   6, 177, 185
worst-case   45
writing 147, 151
written 3, 199
yesterday   26
youhave   148
yourself   114, 120, 130

Made in the USA
Middletown, DE
06 January 2023

21364621R00177